12 - 4 - 1971

For ❤️ at least one of us
will be well versed...
The happiest of
birthdays!
　　　　Much love —
　　　　Nance

J. M. SYNGE
and his world

J. M. SYNGE
and his world

BY ROBIN SKELTON

A STUDIO BOOK

THE VIKING PRESS · NEW YORK

Published in 1971 by The Viking Press, Inc.
625 Madison Avenue, New York, N.Y. 10022

SBN 670–40729–1

Library of Congress catalog card number 75–142147

Printed and bound in Great Britain by Jarrold and Sons Ltd, Norwich, England

To MAURICE GOOD, whose stage portrait of J. M. Synge gives us the living man

Map of Ireland

2 Newtown Villas, Rathfarnham, near Dublin, where J. M. Synge was born

JOHN MILLINGTON SYNGE was born on 16 April 1871 at Rathfarnham, near Dublin, in 2 Newtown Villas, a big grey stucco semi-detached house, with an orchard at the back and a good view of the Dublin Mountains. The Synges were a Protestant family, and strongly enough devoted to their faith to produce five bishops and a quantity of other clergy and missionaries over the years since the first Synge came to Ireland in the seventeenth century. In the eighteenth century the Synges intermarried with the wealthy Hatch family, and thus acquired large estates in Wicklow, Meath and Dublin. Though by the time John Synge was born these estates had somewhat dwindled, they were still large enough to dominate the moral horizons of the family, and to affect the choice of profession for the sons. Robert, Synge's eldest brother, though trained initially as an engineer, at first managed and then owned estates in Argentina. The second son Edward became a land agent, first for the family estates in Wicklow, and later also for Lord Gormanstown. Samuel, the third son, entered the Church and became a missionary in China. Their father John Hatch Synge was a lawyer who specialized in land conveyance. Landlordism combined with Protestantism to form the narrow and rigorous creed of the Synges.

The Synge family

7

The Reverend and Mrs Robert
Traill, Synge's maternal
grandparents, who lived in
Schull, Co. Cork

J. M. Synge's father, John
Hatch Synge, who died a year
after his youngest son was born

J. M. Synge aged one

Protestantism was also the creed of the female line of John Synge's ancestry. His mother was the daughter of Robert Traill, who, born in County Antrim, combined the harsh faith of his inheritance with the passionate zealotry of the evangelical movement, and 'waged war against popery in its thousand forms of wickedness' (his own words) as the rector of Schull in County Cork. He waged the war so aggressively, indeed, that on occasions he found it advisable to ask the police for protection against his parishioners, just as the Reverend Alexander Synge, the playwright's uncle, found it necessary when on the Aran Islands to arrange for armed protection for the fishing vessel which he owned and operated in competition with the islanders.

John Hatch Synge died of the smallpox in 1872 and Mrs Synge moved house to 4 Orwell Park, Rathgar, to live next door to her widowed mother. There she preached her father's doctrines of sin and damnation to her children, and early introduced her youngest son to the idea of Hell. This was for him a traumatic experience. In the middle nineties, as a young man in Paris, he wrote in a series of autobiographical notes, 'I was painfully timid and while still very young the idea of Hell took a fearful hold on me. One night I thought I was irretrievably

9

Leeson Street, Dublin: here Synge commenced his education at Mr Herrick's Classical and English School in the 1870s

damned and cried myself to sleep in vain yet terrified efforts to form a conception of eternal pain. In the morning I renewed my lamentations and my mother was sent for. She comforted me with the assurance that the Holy Ghost was convicting me of sin and thus preparing me for ultimate salvation. This was a new idea and I rather approved.' Though comforted at that time, his fears did not entirely go. He confesses in his autobiographical notes that 'Religion remained a difficulty and occasioned terror to me for many years,' and reflects that 'the well-meant but extraordinary cruelty of introducing the idea of Hell into the imagination of a nervous child has probably caused more misery than many customs that the same people send missionaries to eradicate.'

Early childhood   Lacking a father from the age of one, John Synge was inevitably very much dependent upon his mother and grandmother for his understanding of the world about him. He was a sickly child much troubled by asthma and, after four years of irregular school attendance, first at Mr Herrick's Classical and English School at 4 Leeson Street, Dublin, and later at Bray, he was taught at home by a tutor who came three times a week. His summer holidays provided as little opportunity for mingling with children of different backgrounds and persuasions as did his schooldays. After 1872 they were usually spent in a rented house in Greystones, then a small fishing village. It is significant that one of the houses they used, Castle Kevin, was a boycotted one. Mrs Synge, however, had no hesitations on this score. Her political views were as extreme as her religious ones.

10

The Synge family in 1885. From left to right: Samuel, Annie, Mrs Synge, Robert, John and Edward

'Boycotting' a tradesman, Co. Mayo

In this she was representative of a class that was shortly to die out in Ireland, and was, at the time of Synge's boyhood, embattled and under siege. Michael Davitt's Land League had been founded in 1879, and in 1880 Charles Stewart Parnell, the recalcitrant son of another Protestant Wicklow family, introduced the strategy of boycotting unjust or tyrannous landlords. Evictions continued in spite of opposition, however, and when John Synge was fourteen years old his brother Edward was engaged in evicting tenants on the estates of which he had charge in Counties Cavan, Mayo and Wicklow. In 1887, when John was sixteen, Edward evicted Hugh Carey, the sole support of his two sisters, one of whom was simple-minded, from his cottage on the Synge estate of Glanmore. The eviction was brutal enough to cause angry reports in the *Freeman's Journal* which years later was to take such exception to some of Synge's plays. Some days after the eviction Edward Synge burned the cottage to the ground, and the Synge name became as unpopular in Wicklow as it had become earlier in Aran. John and his mother did not see eye to eye on the morality and justice of these practices, but she answered his objections by asking, 'What would become of us if our tenants in Galway stopped paying the rents?' She saw the situation, moreover, in religious terms. The peasants were Catholics and the majority of landlords Protestants: to deny the landlords their rights of ownership and to permit their tenants to defy them was to invite the triumph of papacy.

12

Charles Stewart Parnell in 1880, the year in which he took up the fight against unjust landlords and introduced the technique of boycotting

The Triple Alliance: Famine, Eviction and Coercion marching in triumph through desolated Ireland, a cartoon of the 1880s

Eviction scenes. The battering-ram is used against peasants' cottages

By the age of sixteen John Synge had, to some extent, managed to develop his own sense of values, and had released himself from the grip of the family faith. This freedom had not been gained without difficulty, however, and, as a young man in his middle twenties, Synge himself attempted to chart the course his early life had taken.

Natural history

Being prevented from most forms of exercise by his poor health, Synge early developed a taste for walking, and with his brother Samuel would wander the woods of Rathfarnham near his home. At the age of ten he became friendly with a female cousin of his own age, Florence Ross, and together they looked after 'a large establishment of pets – rabbits, pigeons, guinea pigs, canaries, dogs'. Their interest in natural history was encouraged by gifts of books. Emulating the as yet unborn Playboy who, according to his father, was 'a man you'd see stretched half the day in the brown ferns', who spent much time 'fooling over little birds he had', and who lay hidden in the sticks watching the passing girls, 'shooting out his sheeps eyes between the little twigs and leaves' – John Synge 'used to hide in bushes to watch with amorous fellowship the mere movements of the birds'. Together, he and Florence 'bought a ten-shilling telescope, which led to trouble afterwards'. He does not tell us the nature of the trouble, but one may suppose that it arose from a suspicion that more came in for scrutiny than was altogether respectable. This was the happiest period of Synge's boyhood. He found it 'admirable in every way'.

His contentment was, however, temporary. The following summer his girlfriend turned her affections elsewhere and he was 'stunned with horror' and fretted himself ill 'in lonely corners'. Although the year afterwards the friendship renewed itself and he became clumsily enamoured of her, and used to 'kiss the chair she had sat on and kiss the little notes' she sent him, the first temporary rejection affected him profoundly. Still in ill health, but possibly also troubled by fears of further rejections, he came to a decision. 'Without knowing, or, as far as I can remember, hearing anything about doctrines of heredity I surmised that unhealthy parents should have unhealthy children – my rabbit breeding may have put the idea into my head. Therefore, I said, I am unhealthy, and if I marry I will have

Illustration from Darwin's *The Zoology of the Voyage of H.M.S. Beagle*

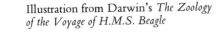

The Dargle, Co. Wicklow. 'Still south I went and west and south again,
Through Wicklow from the morning till the night,
And far from cities, and the sites of men. . . .' *Prelude*

unhealthy children. But I will never create beings to suffer as I am suffering so I
will never marry. I do not know how old I was when I came to this decision,
but I was between thirteen and fifteen and it caused me horrible misery.'

It was the logical turn of mind revealed here that caused him to suffer the next
emotional crisis of his boyhood, and led him to abandon for ever the religious
beliefs of his family. 'When I was about fourteen,' he wrote in 1896–8, 'I obtained
a book of Darwin's. It opened in my hands at a passage where he asks how can we
explain the similarity between a man's hand and a bird's or bat's wings except
by evolution. I flung the book aside and rushed out into the open air – it was
summer and we were in the country – the sky seemed to have lost its blue and the
grass its green. I lay down and writhed in an agony of doubt. My studies showed
me the force of what I read, [and] the more I put it from me the more it rushed
back with new instances and power. Till then I had never doubted and never
conceived that a sane and wise man or boy could doubt. I had of course heard of

Religious
doubts

17

The first excursion for the summer season of the Dublin Naturalists' Field Club, in which Synge took part. Synge's name appears on the membership list as Syne

atheists but as vague monsters that I was unable to realize. It seemed that I was become in a moment the playfellow of Judas. Incest and parricide were but a consequence of the idea that possessed me. My memory does not record how I returned home nor how long my misery lasted. I only know that I got the book out of the house as soon as possible and kept it out of sight, saying to myself logically enough that I was not yet sufficiently advanced in science to weigh his arguments, so I would do better to reserve his work for future study. In a few weeks or days I regained my composure, but this was the beginning. Soon afterwards I turned my attention to works of Christian evidence, reading them at first with pleasure, soon with doubt, and at last in some cases with derision. . . . By the time I was sixteen or seventeen I had renounced Christianity. . . . The story is easily told, but it was a terrible experience. By it I laid a chasm between my present and my past and between myself and my kindred and friends. Till I was twenty-three I never met or at least knew a man or woman who shared my opinions.'

Forced into comparative solitude and independence of mind, first by his health and later by his beliefs, John Synge sought for a belief or a cause in which there might be some form of self-fulfilment. He joined the Dublin Naturalists' Field Club on its foundation in 1886 but never gave any papers. His interest in the natural world became more romantic than scientific, and he found that 'the forces which rid me of theological mysticism reinforced my innate feeling for the profound mysteries of life.' He derived 'a strange sense of enchantment' and delight from 'furze bushes and rocks and flooded streams and strange mountain fogs and sunshine.' He felt on one occasion a strange terror at the 'fearful and genuine hypnotic influence' exerted upon him by the mysterious appearances of the natural world. He read Wordsworth with passion. It was music rather than poetry to which he turned at this time, however, and in 1887 he began studying the violin under Patrick Griffith in Dublin.

Music

I beg to acknowledge, with thanks, receipt of one Guinea, from John M. Synge Esq for six violin lessons given him. (latest on Oct 25^{d} '88) £1. 1.

P. J. Griffith.

24 LONGWOOD AVENUE, SOUTH CIRCULAR ROAD, DUBLIN.

Patrick Griffith's bill for violin lessons given J. M. Synge in 1888

Synge's violin and bow. 'In my sixteenth year everything changed. I took to the violin and the study of literature with wild excitement and lost almost completely my interest in natural science, although the beauty of nature influenced me more than ever.' *A Notebook of 1896–8*

19

In the following March he was obliged temporarily to abandon this enthusiasm to study for the entrance examination to Trinity College, which he passed without distinction. He wrote later that he gained little from Trinity. 'All my time was given to the violin and vague private reading, and the work for my examinations received just enough attention to attain the pass standard.' He may, however, have underestimated the influence of his college years. Although he had as his tutor his mother's cousin, Anthony Traill, a man not particularly noted for either refinement or learning, but who nevertheless became in the fullness of time the Provost of the College, and although he continued to live at home rather than take rooms, his studies enabled him to escape even more completely from his family background. He wrote himself, 'Soon after I had relinquished the Kingdom of God I began to take a real interest in the kingdom of Ireland. My politics went round from a vigorous and unreasoning loyalty to a temperate Nationalism. Everything Irish became sacred . . . and had a charm that was neither quite human nor divine, rather perhaps as if I had fallen in love with a goddess, although I had still sense

Irish
Nationalism

Trinity College, Dublin, where Synge studied
from 1888 to 1892. Above, College Green; left,
the library; right, Synge's tutor Anthony Traill;
and below, his library card

No. 208 Trinity College, Dublin.
5
18th of November, 18 91.
John M. Synge
is admitted to read in the Library from the date of
this Ticket to the 31st of December, 18 91.
Dr. Traill   T. V. Keenan,
                              Asst. Librarian.

The West door of the twelfth-century cathedral of Saints Peter and Paul, and right, the church and graveyard, Glendalough, Co. Wicklow. 'At the end of the Upper Lake at Glendalough one is quite shut off from the part that has been spoiled by civilization. . . .'

enough not to personify Erin in the patriotic verse I now sought to fabricate. Patriotism gratifies Man's need for adoration and has therefore a peculiar power upon the imaginative sceptic.'

He fed his need for adoration by taking a great interest in Irish antiquities, and visiting all those available to him in and near Dublin, making sketches of a number of ancient doorways as well as one of a round tower, and copying several Gaelic inscriptions. He also became engrossed in the poetry of *The Spirit of the Nation* and thought that crude but influential patriotic verse excellent, at least for a while.

Mrs Synge's disquiet

His mother, while complacent over her son Edward's continuing evictions of Mayo peasants, was disturbed by her son John's increasing unorthodoxy. She wrote to Robert that he was longing for the lectures to stop so that he might take up his music lessons again, and added, 'Oh! that I could say his soul is in health. I hope you pray for him, the only one of my dear children a stranger to God.' She was disturbed by his 'always composing little airs and making out accompaniments for them on the piano, which I have to play', and in April she wrote to Robert: 'He leads a queer solitary life poor boy. He plays his fiddle a great deal and reads and takes a walk. I wonder what he will turn into by and by. He is a great burden on my heart, but the Lord says, "Cast thy burden on me."'

22

Castle Kevin, Co. Wicklow, the boycotted house in which the Synge family spent many of their summer holidays

Atheism

In fact she chose in the winter of 1889 to cast her burden upon her minister. The result of the minister's discussion with her son was, however, unhelpful to her cause. John at last openly admitted his loss of faith and asserted that he would no longer go through the hypocritical formula of attending church. His mother was deeply distressed and the remainder of his family thereafter regarded him as an alien. His denial of Christianity caused hardly more unease than his enthusiasm for music. When he revealed his intention to make music his profession his mother, in desperation, sent Harry Stephens, her daughter Annie's husband, to talk him out of it. Harry warned him that all the men who make music a profession take to drink and that musicians were not 'a nice set of men'. To John Synge, desperately weary of the puritanical atmosphere of his family, this may not have been the most effective argument to have put forward.

This particular crisis was caused by John's beginning, in November 1889, to attend lectures in musical theory at the Royal Academy of Music. He continued his studies there for three years, studying, in addition to musical theory, the violin and composition. In 1890 Mrs Synge once again revealed her sense of the importance of family solidarity. When Harry and Annie Stephens moved house to Crosthwaite Park, Kingstown (now Dun Laoghaire) she moved into the house beside them, and a connecting door was created between the two houses. Here, with that tenacity of purpose which later characterized her son John, she continued to press the Bible upon him, aided by Samuel who was now a student of divinity. John, however, went his own way. In January 1891 he joined the orchestra of the Academy, and played in a concert in March. Mrs Synge was not comforted by such success. He narrowly passed his next examinations at Trinity but worked more assiduously for a scholarship examination in counterpoint. He studied *Studies the* Hebrew and Irish, though the only Irish text used was, in his own words 'a *Irish language* crabbed version of the New Testament', and his teacher 'seemed to know nothing, or at least care nothing, about the old literature of Ireland, or the fine folk-tales and folk-poetry of Munster and Connacht.' Nevertheless he added to this knowledge of Ireland's past by picking up books and pamphlets in the stalls and shops on Bachelors' Walk and Aston's Quay where Leopold Bloom was later to contemplate *Sweets of Sin*. He played again in a concert at the Molesworth Hall in January 1892, and was awarded the scholarship in counterpoint on 16 March. He was now reading *The Children of Lir* and *Diarmuid and Grania* in Irish. That summer he spent his holidays with the family at Castle Kevin, a boycotted house not far from Glanmore Castle, the Synge family seat, which he had once visited three years earlier. The local populace were resentful of their presence and the local policeman thought it wise to pay a daily visit. Mrs Synge

Crosthwaite Park, Kingstown, where the Synge family lived from 1890 to 1906

The Synge family seat: Glanmore Castle, Co. Wicklow. It was built by J.M. Synge's great-grandfather, Francis Synge, at the beginning of the nineteenth century, and belonged to J.M. Synge's uncle, another Francis, during his lifetime. It has since been pulled down

Cœlestia Canimus

The coat of arms of the Synge family

must have been unperturbed, for Castle Kevin became the regular summer retreat for some years.

Her son John, however, was more aware of the implications of the desolate wilderness of the garden with its broken walls and decaying greenhouses. Writing about it later in the *Manchester Guardian* he said: 'Everyone is used in Ireland to the tragedy that is bound up with the lives of farmers and fishing people; but in this garden one seemed to feel the tragedy of the landlord class also, and of the innumerable old families that are quickly dwindling away. These owners of the land are not much pitied at the present day, or much deserving of pity; and yet one cannot quite forget that they are the descendants of what was at one time, in the eighteenth century, a high-spirited and highly-cultivated aristocracy. The broken green-houses and mouse-eaten libraries that were designed and collected by men who voted with Grattan, are perhaps as mournful in the end as the four mud walls that are so often left in Wicklow as the only remnants of a farmhouse.' Opposed to the tenets of his own family and class, he nevertheless recognized that

26

Glanmore Castle: a distant view

A Wicklow cottage

the Protestant ascendancy had once been cultivated and to a degree socially enlightened. In his walks through Wicklow that summer and in following years he became intimately aware of the life of the Wicklow peasants and of his own family's involvement in the area. In his essay 'The People of the Glens' he described meeting an octogenarian who told him of the past. '"There are two branches of the Synges in the County Wicklow," he said, and then went on to tell me fragments of folk-lore connected with my forefathers. How a lady used to ride through Roundwood "on a curious beast" to visit an uncle of hers in Roundwood Park, and how she married one of the Synges and got her weight in gold – eight stone of gold – as her dowry; stories that referred to events which took place more than a hundred years ago.' It is clear that the Synges of the past were more to his taste than those of the present.

In September 1892 he returned to Crosthwaite Park and settled down to composing music and analysing concertos and symphonies by Mozart. He sent a somewhat Wordsworthian poem to the *Irish Monthly*, but it was very properly rejected, though an equally Wordsworthian petrarchan sonnet on Glencullen was published in *Kottabos* for the Hilary term of 1893. He was accorded the dubious distinction of a pass degree on 15 December 1892, and again returned to Crosthwaite Park to write music, perform in concerts, and occasionally play his violin to the family and their friends. He took no part in politics. The fall of Parnell in 1890 and his death in 1891 seem not to have aroused him at the time, and though his arguments with his family occasionally resulted in outbursts of temper, he appears to have grown so used to his intellectual isolation as to have been relatively untroubled by it.

The calm was not to last. Cherry Matheson, the daughter of a leader of the Plymouth Brethren, first met him at Castle Kevin. Later her family moved to Crosthwaite Park and John fell in love with her. His affection was returned, but she was an unquestioning believer in her father's religion, and could not bring herself to think of marrying an atheist. Deeply disturbed by this rejection, and by the way in which his intellectual convictions prevented the fulfilment of his emotional needs, John must have been more than grateful when Mary Synge, an English cousin of his father's and a concert pianist, came on a visit and persuaded the family that he should go to Germany to continue his musical studies. Excited at the prospect he took up the study of German once again, and planned the writing of an opera on Eileen Aruine. At the end of July he left Ireland for London, where he met Mary Synge, and together they travelled to Coblenz. It was as much a turning-point in his life as that day when he discovered Darwin and found himself spiritually and intellectually as far from his family as he was now to become physically.

First Love

Synge arrived at the boarding-house run by the four von Eiken sisters, Hedwig, Emma, Claire and Valeska, just above Oberwerth on the Rhine, on 21 July 1893. His immediate reactions may be judged from the entry in his diary for the following day: 'The day of Valeska!' Valeska was the youngest of the sisters and immediately became his confidante and German teacher, and teased him by calling him 'Holy Moses' because this was an expression he often used. She became 'Gorse'. He found her company totally delightful and was able to talk freely to her of his thoughts and feelings, and discuss his love for Cherry Matheson whom she nicknamed 'The Holy One'. Moreover, in this society he found his musical ambitions were regarded seriously. He wrote to his mother asking for permission and money to stay longer than the two months originally planned. Although she agreed and sent him the money, she was irritated by his enthusiasm for his new friends, and recorded in her diary her receipt of a 'long letter from poor Johnnie. . . . Curious letter attributing his unsociableness to his narrow bringing up and warning me!'

John left Oberwerth at the end of his violin lessons in December and went to Würzburg for further studies. There his loneliness led him to correspond regularly with the von Eikens, and he visited them for a week's holiday at Easter 1894. Back again in Würzburg he began again to write poems and even made notes for a play in which a young scion of the landlord class returns to Ireland from Paris and marries a daughter of one of the peasant families on the estate. He was beginning to have doubts about his musical career, having discovered that he had neither the taste nor the self-confidence for solo performances. He talked it all over with Valeska when he spent another twelve days at Oberwerth in June 1894 before returning to Ireland, Cherry Matheson and a family holiday with the Stephens in Wicklow.

Back in Crosthwaite Park and again subjected to Samuel's missionary endeavours, Synge became very depressed. The year abroad had isolated him even further from his family, and though, when Cherry Matheson joined them all at Castle Kevin for a fortnight, he enjoyed long talks with her about Wordsworth and their favourite painters, showing his enthusiasm and interest by the extreme rapidity of his talk, it was clear that he was eager once again to escape. His nervousness was such that when on one occasion his small nephew Edward Stephens came into the room as he was playing his violin to Cherry, he abandoned his instrument and left the room. Though this was a small enough disturbance, it loomed so large in his mind that later he incorporated it in an exaggerated form in *Vita Vecchia*, and told how the hero dreamed of playing the violin to 'a young girl of the Catholic Church' and of being interrupted by a 'crowd of people' who 'rushed into the room with such noise and disturbance' that he stopped playing and threw his fiddle to the floor 'with the horror of nightmare'.

In isolating this one incident as an emotional crisis, as he also isolated his memories of fearing damnation, discovering Darwin and being rejected by Florence Ross, he was, perhaps, rather finding an image in which he could sum up a state of mind than accurately identifying the precise occasion at which it came into being. Nevertheless, that summer, he decided to abandon music as a career, and in October left again for Oberwerth, where he spent a few days before travelling onwards to Paris where he intended to study at the Sorbonne and earn his living as a teacher of English. He found a room with the Arbeau family at 94 rue Lafayette. M. Arbeau, a professional cook, supplemented his income by making and selling tooth powder, and his wife, with some female assistance, made women's hats. It was a considerable change from the world of the von Eikens, to whom he wrote frequently, and at least once so informally that Valeska felt it necessary to chide him for addressing her by her Christian name alone and not as Miss Valeska. Middle-class respectability opposed him as always.

Abandons music

The visiting card of Fräulein von Eiken, in whose house
Synge stayed in 1893, and a bill given Synge by the
von Eiken sisters

J. M. Synge on 31 December 1895

Paris, Avenue de l'Opéra. Synge spent the greater part of the years 1894–1902 in Paris, and retained a room there until March 1903

The winter of 1894–5 was a cold one, and some days he was obliged to stay in his attic bed in order to keep warm. Nevertheless, he began to seek out friends. He joined a students' club for this purpose, and he also settled down to writing poems and articles and teaching students. He moved to another room in 2 rue Leopold Robert in April, and in June he found a girl-friend in one of his students, Thérèse Beydon, a Protestant art teacher and ardent feminist. To her, as earlier to Florence Ross, Cherry Matheson and Valeska von Eiken, he was able to open his heart. With women he was always more at ease than with men. He found himself able to entertain them with his wit and became in their company far more articulate than he ever was with men. John Masefield said of him later; 'His talk to women had a lightness and charm. It was sympathetic; never assertive as the hard, brilliant Irish intellect so often is.' Sympathy and charm were not always quite enough,

33

Paris, Bibliothèque Nationale

however. In an early draft of his first play (*When the Moon Has Set*) Synge included a letter of advice left to the hero by his dead uncle. It contained the following words:

'My life has gone to ruin because I misunderstood love and because I was scrupulous when I should have been strong. I treated women as if they were gods and they treated me as if I might be damned for their amusement.

'When I was a young man I read Goethe and Heine, the men who were most prominent in literature at that time, and I learned things from them that made the women of my country avoid me because they were pious, and the men because they were stupid. If you love a woman subdue her.'

Whether or not Synge attempted to subdue Cherry Matheson on his return to Ireland in the summer of 1895, he did not succeed in converting her to his way of thinking, though he traded on their mutual interest in art, taking her to the National Gallery and the Sketching Club. She later described him saying to her, 'It is very amusing to me coming back to Ireland to find myself looked upon as a Pariah because I don't go to church and am not orthodox, while in Paris among the students I am looked upon as a saint because I don't do the things they do.'

He continued his studies of philosophy and political thought. He had attended lectures by the anarchist Sébastien Faure in Paris in June, and throughout July and August he studied Petrie on Irish antiquities and Herbert Spencer, and renewed his interest in the Irish language and took Italian lessons. On his return to Paris early in the new year he took Room 47 at the Hotel Corneille and spent a month there before setting off on an Italian tour on 3 February. He was enchanted by Rome, where he stayed in a pension at 73 Aureliana, and wrote an article on the

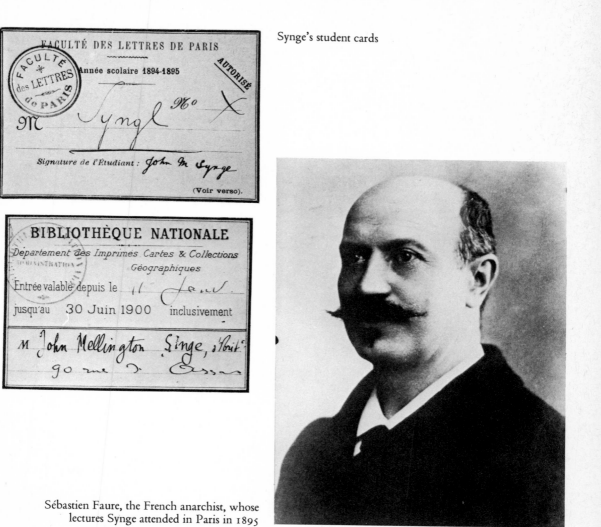

Synge's student cards

Sébastien Faure, the French anarchist, whose lectures Synge attended in Paris in 1895

35

Visit to Italy anti-Government demonstrations arising out of the Italian defeats in the Abyssinian War; this he sent to the *Irish Times*, but it was not published. He became friendly with an American girl, a Miss Capps, who stayed at the same pension, but, as before, found that his atheism made real intimacy impossible. He lent her Renan's *Vie de Jesus*, thus emulating Cherry Matheson, who insisted on lending him books of an opposite tendency, but the friendship did not prosper. He moved to Florence on 1 May where he continued to read Petrarch, some of whose *Sonnets to Laura* he was later to translate, and met Marie Antoinette Zdanowska, a devoutly Roman Catholic art student. She directed his attention to various theological works, and he told her about Cherry. A third boarder in the pension, Hope Rea, an English girl working on a book about Tuscan art, was rationalist in attitude and took Synge's part in the arguments. He corresponded with both girls for several years, and, to Mrs Synge's concern, remained close friends with the 'modern sceptic'.

Left, Rome, Campo dei Fiori

Above, Florence, where Synge spent
the whole of May 1896, and right, the
visiting card of Hope Rea, inscribed
with a note of thanks

*with many thanks — to
Il Figlinolo —*

Miss Hope Rea.

60. Belsize Park Gardens. N.W.

On his return to Paris he stayed briefly at the Hôtel de l'Univers from where he wrote to Cherry proposing marriage. He was refused. He returned to Ireland on 1 July, and immediately abandoned Crosthwaite Park for Wicklow where he walked and fished and wandered, gathering, consciously or unconsciously, material for his future work. He made one more attempt to persuade Cherry to marry him in October, and poured out his feelings in letters to Thérèse Beydon and Hope Rea who were sympathetic, and also to his mother who was deeply distressed at his misery. Cherry remained adamant. He returned to Paris in October after lunching with Hope Rea in London, and there, in the Hotel Corneille, he settled down once again to the composing of poems filled with agony and despair, to the writing of prose notes about his life and beliefs, and to the study of Socialism. Socialism was not a subject that endeared itself to his mother, who wondered if she should continue to support him financially in his folly.

First meeting with W.B. Yeats

It was on 21 December 1896 that Synge met W.B. Yeats. He had published nothing since the sonnet in *Kottabos* three years earlier, and, according to Yeats, had nothing to show for all his work but 'one or two poems and impressionist essays'. Yeats and Maud Gonne were at that time busy founding the Irish League or L'Association Irlandaise, whose object was to fight for Irish independence and enlist the aid of Irish Nationalists in France for this purpose. Synge was in the mood to involve himself in politics. Though he had almost certainly voted against

Membership card of the Democratic Federation, designed by William Morris

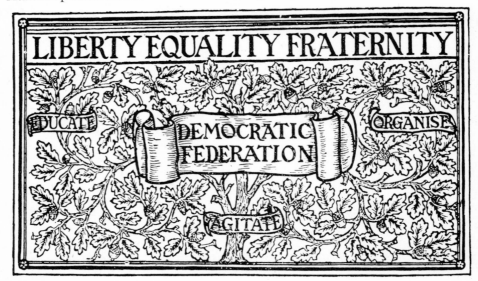

W.B. Yeats

Maud Gonne, a photograph inscribed 'To Mr Synge with kindest regards' in 1897

Home Rule in the Irish election of 1895, in the belief that it would lead to religious disturbances of a severe kind, he considered himself both a Nationalist and a Socialist. He had read the *Communist Manifesto* and several works on Socialism and Anarchism as well as the works of William Morris. The Irish League held its first meeting on New Year's Day 1897 in Maud Gonne's apartment. Maud was now living in Paris, as her agitation on behalf of the peasantry of the West and her incitement of them to band together to defy their landlords had obliged her to flee Ireland under threat of arrest. One of the most beautiful women of her time, she was also one of the most effective speech-makers, and her passion for the cause was unlimited. Synge attended the weekly meetings of the League until he left Paris on 13 May, and it may have been at one of these meetings that Yeats advised Synge to visit the Aran Islands and 'express a life that has never found expression', rather than directly on their first encounter as Yeats implied, which seems improbable.

The Irish League

39

Synge did not, however, visit Aran on his return to Ireland. Nor did he remain a member of the Irish League. He sent Maud Gonne his resignation on 6 April 1897, on the grounds that he so disapproved of the conduct of the journal, *Irlande Libre*, that his presence as a full member of the League would prove to be disruptive. 'I wish', he wrote, 'to work in my own way for the cause of Ireland, and I shall never be able to do so if I get mixed up with a revolutionary and semimilitary movement.' But he was willing to continue to attend meetings as a spectator and gave his opinion and help whenever they were required; and this, indeed, he did. His mother reported to Robert that he was convinced that the spread of *Socialist* Socialism in England would cause Ireland 'to come to her own' and result in *sympathies* 'equality and no more grinding down of the poor'. She came to the conclusion that she would no longer give him money 'to go and live in Paris idle'. He has nearly £40 of his own now, and he can do what he likes with that. It makes him fancy he is independent which is a very great mistake.'

In June Synge came face to face with actual evidence of the new spirit in Ireland. The Unionist celebrations in Dublin of Queen Victoria's Diamond Jubilee were the occasion for a Nationalist demonstration in which James Connolly led a mock funeral procession for John Bull down Sackville (now O'Connell) Street to be met by police baton charges. Synge watched it all.

J. M. Synge in 1897, in the grounds of Castle Kevin. 'A stone's throw from an old house where I spent several summers in County Wicklow, there was a garden that had been left to itself for fifteen or twenty years. . . .' *A Landlord's Garden in County Wicklow*

Synge with his pointer dog Ben, a photograph taken by his nephew, E.M. Stephens

Glenmalure, Co. Wicklow

In July he went with his family once more to Castle Kevin. In August, however, they moved to a house on the Parnell estate at Avondale, and Synge saw the great Parnell mansion empty, and the trees partly felled, all evidence of the fall and ruin of Ireland's sometime 'Chief'.

Wanderings in Wicklow

To these images of unrest and ruin were added those of the wildest parts of Wicklow. He became familiar with those wild glens and desolate places whose names bring music to his poems, essays and plays: Glenmalure, Glen MacNass, Aughavanna, Annamoe. On his return to Dublin in September he added another series of impressions. He had already begun to read the work of Yeats: *The Wanderings of Oisin, The Countess Cathleen, The Land of Heart's Desire, The Celtic Twilight* and *The Secret Rose*. Now, at the insistence of his Paris friend Stephen MacKenna, he began to add to his understanding of the world of the occult. In

42

Glen MacNass, Co. Wicklow. '. . . Glenmacnas and Glenmalure where after a stormy night's rain the whole valley is filled with a riot of waterfalls. Sometimes these sudden rainfalls are followed by a singularly beautiful morning and then each of these glens can be seen at its moment of most direct and wonderful colour [and] beauty.' *A Notebook of 1907*

J. M. Synge, in the period before
he adopted a wig

Paris he had studied the *Proceedings of the Society for Psychical Research*, and in company with Yeats and Maud Gonne, had seen 'manifestations'. Now he explored mysticism and theosophy. In October he even went with A E to a meeting of the Theosophical Society, which Hope Rea was later to join and serve. Then, just at the time when all his ideas were beginning to gather together and form a coherent philosophical and political basis for his work, illness struck. A large lump formed on the side of his neck and his hair began to fall out. He entered Mount Street

Nursing Home on 11 December for an operation. In his essay 'Under Ether' he wrote of the dreams he had under the anaesthetic. 'All secrets were open before me, and simple as the universe to its God. Now and then something recalled my physical life, and I smiled at what seemed a moment of sickly infancy. At other times I felt I might return to earth, and laughed aloud to think what a god I should be among men. For there could be no more terror in my life. I was a light, a joy.' On waking from his dream, and told by a nurse that the operation had been 'satisfactory', he groaned, 'Damn the operation. If I could only remember

44

W.B. Yeats, a caricature by William
Horton, 1898

George Russell (AE), 1903

I'd write books upon books; I'd teach all earth of delight.' The evening of the
following day, after the visitors had gone, he lay back and relaxed. 'From five
o'clock deep drowsiness came over me, and I lay as in lethargy with the lights
carefully lowered. A faint jingle of tram-bells sounded far away, and the voices
of Sunday travellers sometimes broke into my room. I took notice of every familiar
occurrence as if it were something I had come back to from a distant country.
The impression was very strong on me that I had died the preceding day and
come to life again, and this impression has never changed.'

No less than five of the nurses wrote to him after he had left the hospital. They
perhaps knew what he did not, that the lump on the neck was a sign of Hodgkin's
disease, and that he could not expect to live much more than another ten to twelve
years. He left again for Paris on 19 January 1898, pausing *en route* to see Yeats and
Hope Rea in London. He wore a black wig and a soft felt hat and looked, his
mother thought, 'very like a Frenchman'. In fact it was in this year that at last he
began to discover his true role in Ireland's rebirth.

*Return to
Paris*

45

Almost all Synge's writings up to this time had been autobiographical. It seems that he felt compelled to relive and explore all the intellectual and emotional crises of his childhood and youth; he kept a notebook in which he recorded them together with his reflections about them. His poems were equally personal, though in 1895–7, he attempted to give them a fictional framework in a story he called *Vita Vecchia,* and in which he made use of his memories of Rome and Paris. The heart of it was, however, his agony over Cherry Matheson, and this he expressed most directly, together with his childhood conviction that he should not marry, in a poem which he introduced by saying, 'Then my friend to whom I was still desolately faithful, wrote to tell me that her confessor had made her believe that it would be a sin to marry a man who was not a Christian.'

> *I curse my bearing, childhood, youth*
> *I curse the sea, sun, mountains, moon,*
> *I curse my learning, search for truth,*
> *I curse the dawning, night, and noon.*

> *Cold, joyless, I will live, though clean,*
> *Nor by marriage mould to earth*
> *Young lives to see what I have seen,*
> *To curse – as I have cursed – their birth.*

He was now beginning to attempt to transmute the entirely personal into the impersonality of art. He began a novel dealing with the working conditions of nurses which was, presumably, inspired by his memories of the Mount Street Nursing Home, and completed the first draft on 19 February. He was now more than ever interested in things Irish, and attended Professor H. d'Arbois Jubainville's lectures at the Sorbonne in which the ancient Irish civilization was compared with that of Homer's Greece, a comparison he never forgot. He also met Margaret

Margaret Hardon

Hardon, an American art student, a graduate of Wellesley College, whom he nicknamed in his diary 'La Robe Verte', and with whom he was to fall in love.

He left his room in the little St Malo Hotel at 2 rue Odessa at the end of April, and back in Dublin, found that his mother had left Crosthwaite Park for a holiday. He occupied the house by himself for a while, then at last took Yeats' advice and

First visit to Aran

set out for Aran. He arrived on Aranmor (Inishmore) on 10 May. He stayed for two weeks at the Atlantic Hotel, where he bought a camera from another visitor, and studied Irish with Martin Coneely who had taught many others and known Sir William Wilde and Petrie. He then moved to Inishmaan and stayed in Patrick MacDonagh's cottage, where he listened to the stories of old Pat Dirane and

46

The Aran Islands, Kilronan Pier. 'There were few passengers; a couple of men going out with young pigs tied loosely in sacking, three or four young girls who sat in the cabin with their heads completely twisted in their shawls, and a builder, on his way to repair the pier at Kilronan, who walked up and down and talked with me.' *The Aran Islands*

John Joice. He left the islands on 25 June, with a number of superb photographs and a notebook full of material. He had found what he had for so long needed.

The notes which Synge made on this and on his subsequent visits to Aran were, of course, reworked and reordered into a book which has long been accepted as a faithful and moving account of life on the islands. It was for Synge, however, something more, and in many passages, some omitted from the book, he clearly reveals that it satisfied emotional and intellectual needs which he had discovered in himself while making his earlier autobiographical studies. He had found an object *Inishmaan* for his adoration. 'With this limestone Inishmaan', he wrote, 'I am in love, and hear with galling jealousy of the various priests and scholars who have lived here before me. They have grown to me as the former lover of one's mistress, horrible existences haunting with dreamed kisses the lips she presses to your own.' He had again 'fallen in love with a goddess'. His emotions were stirred by the beauty of the island girls, and perhaps by one in particular, for he wrote at the close of his first visit, 'One woman has interested me in a way that binds me more than ever to the islands. These women are before convention and share many things with the women of Paris or London who have freed themselves by a desperate personal effort from moral bondage of ladylike persons.' In another place he recorded, 'In moments of loneliness I am drawn to the girls of the island, for even in remote

Dun Conor, the ancient fortification near Synge's 1898 lodging on Inishmaan where a man wanted for murder was once hidden from the police. 'One of the largest Duns, or pagan forts, on the islands, is within a stone's throw of my cottage, and I often stroll up there after a dinner of eggs or salt pork, to smoke drowsily on the stones.'

The Pier. An illustration by Jack B. Yeats for *The Aran Islands*

sympathy with women there is an interchange of emotion that is independent of *The Aran* ideas.' Two of the island girls, Barbara Coneely and Violet Wallace, wrote to *girls* him, but we cannot know if their friendship with him developed into anything more. We can only be sure that in their 'exquisitely bright frankness' he found a marked contrast to the gentility which had obstructed him in his friendships with others.

He found the wildness and humour of the islanders astonishing and enchanting, and wrote with sympathy of the contempt in which they held the law. Opposite Patrick MacDonagh's cottage on Inishmaan was an ancient megalithic fortifica‚ tion in which the islanders had hidden a Connemara man who was being sought by the police for killing his father with the blow of a spade. 'This impulse to protect the criminal', he wrote, 'is universal in the West. It seems partly due to the association between justice and the hated English jurisdiction, but more directly

49

Aran cottages, Inishmaan

Source-material for plays

to the primitive feelings of these people, who are never criminals yet always capable of crime, that a man will not do wrong unless he is under the influence of a passion which is as irresponsible as a storm on the sea. If a man has killed his father, and is already sick and broken with remorse, they can see no reason why he should be dragged away and killed by the law.' In this story he found the germ of *The Playboy of the Western World*, as in a story of Pat Dirane's he found the plot for *In the Shadow of the Glen*, and in several events the basis for *Riders to the Sea*. On Inishmore, during his first few days, Martin Coneely showed him the ruined Church of the Four Beautiful Persons beside which was a holy well, and told him a story of its curing the blindness of a boy. This provided him with one of the basic ingredients of *The Well of the Saints*. It was during a later stay in Aran, in 1900 or 1901, that

The Church of the Four Beautiful Persons, Inishmore

he began a translation from the Gaelic of the Deirdre story. Of all his perfected dramas, only *The Tinker's Wedding* owes nothing to his Aran adventures.

If Aran satisfied his need for an escape from middle-class gentility and provided him with subject-matter for his plays, it also satisfied other and more profound yearnings. In the stories of Pat Dirane he found parallels with Greek myth and with European folk-tales that recalled for him the arguments of Professor Jubainville, and in the simplicity of the islanders' life he must have been reminded of the anarchism of Sébastien Faure. 'It is likely,' he wrote, 'that much of the intelligence and charm of these people is due to the absence of any division of labour, and to the correspondingly wide development of each individual, whose varied knowledge and skill necessitates a considerable activity of mind.' To the charms of the

Aran Island culture

51

Making pampooties: A piece of raw ▶
cowhide, hair outside, is laced over the
toe and round the heel with two ends of
fishing line, brought round and tied
over the instep. The shoes are kept
supple in wear by constant soaking in
water. Synge obtained pairs of
pampooties for the cast of the first
production of *Riders to the Sea* in
order to give the play a
further degree of authenticity

Bringing in the seaweed for kelp, above,
and right, making kelp, a drawing by Jack B.
Yeats. 'In Aran, even manufacture is of
interest.' *The Aran Islands*

52

primitive Anarcho-syndicalist, or even Communist, society was added that of a craftsmanship-orientated community similar to that beloved of William Morris. He wrote of the island man: 'Each man can speak two languages. He is a skilled fisherman, and can manage a curagh with extraordinary nerve and dexterity. He can farm simply, burn kelp, cut out pampooties, mend nets, build and thatch a house, and make a cradle or a coffin. His work changes with the seasons in a way that keeps him free from the dullness that comes to people who have always the same occupation. The danger of his life on the sea gives him the alertness of a primitive hunter, and the long nights he spends fishing in his curagh bring him some of the emotions that are thought peculiar to men who have lived with the arts.' In another place he wrote, 'Every article on these islands has an almost

Aran Islanders in a curagh. Synge wrote: 'It gave me a moment of exquisite satisfaction to find myself moving away from civilization in this rude canvas canoe of a model that has served primitive races since men first went on the sea.' *The Aran Islands*

Carrying a curagh on Inisheer

personal character, which gives this simple life, where all art is unknown, something of the artistic beauty of medieval life.'

Synge, while on Aran, noted only those aspects of the island life which fed his own imagination and supported his views. Though well equipped to comment upon the many prehistoric remains, he only touched on them in passing, and while he referred to the hardness of the islanders' life he did so rather with the admiration of the romantic than with the concern of the sociologist. He collected a number of stories, but only recorded those which most obviously supported his view of the ancient nature of the oral culture and emphasized the mythic intensity of the island imagination. He sought to indicate the universality of that which he saw,

An old Galway woman. 'For these people the outrage to the hearth is the supreme catastrophe. They live here in a world of grey, where there are wild rains and mists every week in the year, and their warm chimney corners, filled with children and young girls, grow into the consciousness of each family in a way it is not easy to understand in more civilized places.' *The Aran Islands*

comparing an Aran festival to one in Brittany, and writing of an eviction, 'The outrage to a tomb in China probably gives no greater shock to the Chinese than the outrage to a hearth in Inishmaan gives to the people.' He noted the similarity of one story to that of Hercules and the Shirt of Nessus, and watching the confusion of men and horses in a boat said that 'the hold seemed to be filled with a mass of struggling centaurs'. In Inishmaan he found himself 'forced to believe in a sympathy between man and nature' as he had believed in it in childhood. This sympathy was bred as much of inheritance as circumstance. He saw the Aran world as one of the last relics of ancient primitive civilization. 'These strange men with receding foreheads, high cheek-bones, and ungovernable eyes seem to represent some old type found on these few acres at the extreme border of Europe, where it is only in wild jests and laughter that they can express their loneliness and desolation.' When he published one of Pat Dirane's stories as *A Story from Inishmaan* in the *New Ireland Review* for November 1898, he ended it by saying, 'It is hard to assert at what date such stories as these reached the west. There is little doubt that our heroic tales which show so often their kinship with Grecian myths, date from the pre-ethnic period of the Aryans, and it is easy to believe that some purely secular narratives share their antiquity. Further, a comparison of all the versions will show that we have here one of the rudest and therefore, it may be, most ancient settings of the material.'

Antiquity of Aran stories

In this place he felt himself 'beyond the dwelling place of man' and in touch with a 'world of inarticulate power'. By temperament a natural mystic and romantic, he had for long found his imagination cramped by a religion which was little more than a codification of class morality. In Aran he found a belief in the miraculous and supernatural which invigorated his imagination. He found himself believing that he could understand the cries of the gulls and, one night, after a dream of ecstasy and frenzy in which he was 'swept away in a whirlwind' of music, he found himself convinced 'that there is a psychic memory attached to certain neighbourhoods'. He recorded with obvious pleasure a story of the faery in which the narrator referred to 'them Protestants who don't believe in any of these things and do be making fun of us', and after telling of a recital of the *Love Songs of Connaught* wrote, 'It seemed like a dream that I should be sitting here among these men and women listening to this rude and beautiful poetry that is filled with the oldest passions of the world.' He described a woman as being at one time 'a simple peasant' and yet at another as 'looking out at the world with a sense of prehistoric disillusion'. He found 'divine simplicity' in the 'ancient Gaelic' of Inishmaan, and wondered if there was not a connection 'between the wild mythology that is accepted on the islands and the strange beauty of the women'.

In the Aran Islands he found his vision of human nature and of the human predicament. Haunted by thoughts of mortality, he saw in the endless battle of the islanders with the elements and their constant nearness to sudden death a parable of the human condition. In their wildness and savagery he saw the vitality that civilization had minimized with its moral codifications and in their ancient culture, their stories and mythic understanding of the natural world, he perceived a kind of knowledge that lay deeper than that of the intellect. When he left Aran after his first visit on 25 June, to stay with Lady Gregory at Coole Park, he had the themes of his drama already within him, though he did not himself realize it for some time.

Lady Augusta Gregory

Lady Gregory's house at Coole Park

It was W. B. Yeats who suggested that Lady Gregory should ask Synge to stay for a while. She had not met him though she had seen him in the distance on Aranmor where she herself had been collecting folk-tales. In writing her invitation she asked him to see if the people remembered 'the names of Aengus and Mannanan and the like, and if they know anything of the Dundonians, as I have heard the De Dananns called'. Later, when she was able to read the manuscript of his book aloud to Yeats, she wished him to leave out the actual names of the islands and leave the localities vague so as to give the book 'a curious dreaminess', and advised him to add more material on faery belief and the words of some of the keens and cradle songs. Synge did not remove the place-names. Aran was for him much more than a source book for Irish folklore, and its actuality and solidity was as essential a part of his vision of it as its superstitions, myths and mysteries.

At the time Synge visited Coole Park on 27 June 1898, Lady Gregory, the widow of an ex-Governor of Ceylon who had become passionately concerned in Irish Nationalism, together with Edward Martyn, a wealthy and intensely Catholic Galway landowner, and the already well-established George Moore and W. B. Yeats, was planning the foundation of an Irish Literary Theatre, whose first production was to be Yeats' *The Countess Cathleen* and Martyn's *The Heather Field*. Synge visited Edward Martyn at Tullira Castle five miles away from Coole in the company of Yeats, and took part in some of the discussions of the project. For the first time in his life he was being regarded as one who could make a definite contribution to an Irish cultural renaissance. It was more to his taste than the political movement he had encountered in Paris.

While Yeats was struggling with the practical problems of finding and licensing a theatre, Synge was in Wicklow where he began serious work on his Aran book and sent his first published essay, 'A Story from Inishmaan' off to the *New Ireland Review*. He also made a number of critical observations which reveal that National-ism had now become part of his literary as well as his political credo. 'Goethe's weakness [is] due to his having no national and intellectual mood to interpret. The individual mood is often trivial, perverse, fleeting [but the] national mood [is] broad, serious, provisionally permanent.' Though convinced of this he was not yet certain of his own role in Irish letters, and when he returned to Paris and an

unfurnished room at 90 rue d'Assas he still regarded himself primarily as a critic, though now interested more in commenting upon Irish phenomena than others. Marie Zdanowska and Margaret Hardon were both in Paris and he continued his friendship with the former while falling in love with the latter. His poems of the time are as agonized as previously. He had still not entirely managed to solve the problem of his emotional life and continued work on *Etude Morbide* which he had begun some time earlier. This work, like *Vita Vecchia*, is a study of the psy-chology of its narrator, though it contains no verse and is in journal form. It is the story of a violinist who breaks down during his first solo recital, thus causing his mistress, the Cellianini, to have hysterics and to be taken away to the asylum where she dies. He has also become fond of one of his girl students, the Chouska, to whom he proposes marriage after having been saved from despair and thoughts of suicide, first by reading Thomas à Kempis' *Imitation of Christ* and then by dis-covering in Brittany the simple life of the peasant. The Chouska rejects his pro-posal, saying: 'We dream and marriage would wake us. Do not talk of it. I leave your love not as a thing I renounce, but cling rather to the heaven I know. I have learned in Paris that I am not destined to achieve distinction in my art; you tell me that your poetry is of no value. But be sure that we at least have failed because we feel the inexpressible.'

Part of the trunk of the great copper beech at Coole Park upon which all Lady Gregory's more eminent visitors were required to carve their initials. Among those who did so were George Bernard Shaw, W. B. Yeats, AE, Douglas Hyde, Sean O'Casey and J. M. Synge

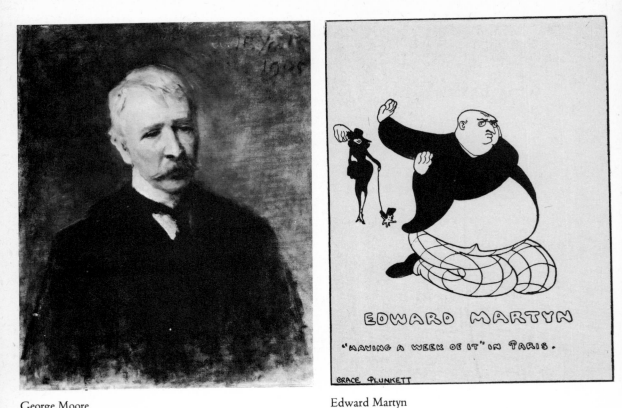

George Moore

Edward Martyn

EDWARD MARTYN

"HAVING A WEEK OF IT" IN PARIS.

GRACE PLUNKETT

Rejection by
Margaret Hardon

That spring Synge proposed to Margaret Hardon and was rejected. He tried again by letter from Dublin in June, but she wrote: 'Please do not delude yourself by any signs in dreams that you consider favourable. You know I have always been interested in you and your work and this winter considered you as a friend. But beyond that there is nothing and never can be.' It seems clear that, again, Synge was dramatizing and magnifying his personal life.

While reading and wrestling with his own identity Synge wrote two reviews for the *Daily Express*, Dublin, one of Maeterlinck's *La Sagesse et le Destinée*, published on 17 December 1898 and the other an article on the work of Anatole le Braz, published on 28 January 1899. He was now studying Breton, and spent a fortnight in Brittany in April where it seems likely that he wrote the Breton entries in the *Etude Morbide* journal. On 8 May he arrived in London *en route* for Dublin, and on that evening the first production of the Irish Literary Theatre opened in Dublin. Martyn's play was applauded, but Yeats' *The Countess*

Tullira Castle, the home of Edward Martyn. Here Martyn, Synge and W.B. Yeats discussed the founding of the Irish Literary Theatre in June 1898

Cathleen, having been already condemned by Cardinal Logue (who had not read it) as being heretical, and also by others, aroused such a storm of disapproval that only the presence of the police whom Yeats had called in to protect the players, enabled the work to be presented. It was a taste of what was to come. Synge went to the performance of 12 May. There is no record of his views. He spent the summer in Wicklow as usual and a few days after his return to Dublin set off again for Aran, arriving on 12 September after two days in Galway. He stayed until 7 October and regained his room in the rue d'Assas on 3 November.

In Dublin the new century began with more trouble; Queen Victoria's visit to the city in April was the occasion for many inflammatory speeches and demonstrations. Synge must have heard talk of it when he returned to Dublin in May and began his summer at Castle Kevin, to which retreat Mrs Synge had thoughtfully invited two respectable girls, both good church workers, for the summer. Synge complained bitterly of this blatant manoeuvre to Stephen MacKenna and

The Irish Literary Theatre

expressed a strong desire for 'a breath of the wickedness of Paris' if only as a relief from missionary conversation. It was with some relief that he returned to Aran in the middle of September. Indeed, he wrote that 'as I sat down on my stool and lit my pipe with the corner of a sod I could have cried out with the feeling of festivity that this return procured me.'

It was during this third visit to Aran that Synge observed the incident which he later used as the basic plot for *Riders to the Sea*:

'Now a man has been washed ashore in Donegal with one pampooty on him, and a striped shirt with a purse in one of the pockets, and a box for tobacco.

'For three days the people here have been trying to fix his identity. Some think it is the man from this island, others think that the man from the south answers the description more exactly. Tonight as we were returning from the slip we met the mother of the man who was drowned from this island, still weeping and looking out over the sea. She stopped the people who had come over from the south island to ask them with a terrified whisper what is thought over there.

'Later in the evening, when I was sitting in one of the cottages, the sister of the dead man came in through the rain with her infant, and there was a long talk about the rumours that had come in. She pieced together all she could remember about his clothes, and what his purse was like, and where he had got it, and the

Return of the fishing boats, Aran Islands

Aran cottage

same of his tobacco box and his stockings. In the end there seemed little doubt that it was her brother.

' "Ah!" she said, "it's Mike sure enough, and please God they'll give him a decent burial." '

It was during this visit to Aran that Synge read in Keating's *Foras Feasa Ar Eirinn: The History of Ireland*, the story of another death by drowning, that of three fishermen who, having accidentally discovered Ireland, brought their wives there from Spain, only to be drowned in the Flood. Their names were Luasnad, Capa and Laighne. This story, too, he later developed into a play.

65

He was still, however, thinking mainly of his Aran book, and on returning to Dublin in the middle of October he bought, at Richard Best's advice, a Blickens-derfer typewriter which had its own wooden case and must have been one of the first portable typewriters made. With this machine he composed all his works, beginning that winter in Paris (to which he returned on 1 November) with a play he later called *When the Moon Has Set*, and with his work on Aran.

When the Moon Has Set was to be the first play Synge completed, and into it, as into *Etude Morbide*, he poured all his convictions and confusions. The basic plot is simple enough. A young man on a walk in the country meets an old madwoman, Mary Costello, who frightens him with her wild talk. He returns to the large country house in which his uncle had just died and learns that the woman had gone mad because in earlier days she had rejected his uncle's love, for religious reasons. He uses this instance and other arguments to persuade his uncle's nurse, a young and beautiful nun, Sister Eileen, to give up the veil and marry him. Finally she discards her habit and puts on 'a green dress cut low at the neck' and agrees to accept his love. The play runs to many drafts and in the earlier ones Synge utilizes passages from *Etude Morbide*, and even arranges for the hero to have a long discus-sion with a violinist who refers to 'a story I have partly told in verse I call *Vita Vecchia*' and to 'the study I call the vale of shadow'. Many of the speeches in early drafts reveal the intensity of Synge's feelings about his upbringing. The hero says: 'The old fashioned Irish conservatism and morality seemed to have evolved a melancholy degeneration worse than anything in Paris.' In another place he maintains: 'The worst vice is slight compared with the guiltiness of a man or woman who defies the central order of the world. . . . The only truth a wave knows is that it is going to break. The only truth a bud knows is that it is going to expand and flower. The only truth we know is that we are a flood of magnificent life the fruit of some frenzy of the earth.' He says to Sister Eileen: 'Far down in below the level of your creed you know that motherhood, the privilege that lifts women up to share in the pain and passion of the earth, is more holy than the vows you have made.' And he writes to a friend of 'the unhealthy women of Ireland who scorn the rules of life and the beauty that is possible and only possible within them'.

When the Moon Has Set began with fragmentary notes in 1896–8, achieved a two-act version by the end of 1901 and a further one-act version in 1902–3. Synge retained the typescripts and worksheets of the play when he tidied up his papers before his death, and clearly intended them to be available for his literary executors to study. He could not ever escape from the effect of his early experiences of rejection, and could not bring himself to discard work into which he had put so much of his early life. In *When the Moon Has Set* (a title not given until 1903) he combined many different personal experiences and concerns together to form a dramatic vehicle for his attitudes towards life, love and death, as he was to do in all his later works. Everything he wrote was to spring directly from his own personal concerns. The green dress of Sister Eileen alludes to Margaret Hardon, 'La Robe Verte', and her attitudes are those of Cherry Matheson and Marie Zdanowska. The hero, in all his manifestations, is the young Synge and also the hero of *Vita Vecchia*. The country house is a conflation of Castle Kevin and the Parnell house.

In 1907, when contemplating publishing a selection of his poems, Synge wrote: 'a man who has made the gradual and conscious expression of his personality in literature the aim of his life has no right to suppress himself any carefully considered work which seemed good enough when it was written.' In the 1908 version of this preface he wrote: 'Many of the older poets, such as Villon and Herrick and Burns, used the whole of their personal life as their material, and the verse written in this way was read by strong men, and thieves, and deacons, not by little cliques only.' This concern to embody his own personal experiences in art was perhaps forced upon him by the necessity to identify and heal psychic wounds. Beginning

J. M. Synge's typewriter and its travelling case. Synge wrote all his works with this machine, only reverting to handwriting for some letters and for notebook work

with obvious and crude transcriptions of experience in the works up to and including *When the Moon Has Set*, he developed the much more sophisticated autobiographical constructions of *The Aran Islands* and the early essays, and then a drama whose bases in personal experience and private obsessions are disguised from all but those who choose to explore, with the aid of the materials he left behind him, the creative procedures of its author.

During the winter of 1900–1 in Paris Synge met R. Barry O'Brien, the editor of *The Speaker*, for whom he wrote a review of the *Poems of Geoffrey Keating* published on 8 December. He wrote five other reviews for *The Speaker* over the years 1901–4. In April 1901 he published another piece about Aran, 'The Last Fortress of the Celt', in *The Gael*. When he returned to Ireland in May 1901 he had also completed drafts of the first three sections of *The Aran Islands*. The gland on his neck had swollen again, but he decided against another operation. Mrs Synge was terribly distressed by both his physical and spiritual condition, but, perseveringly, invited two more religiously minded young ladies for the summer holidays at Castle Kevin. They may well have been of some service to Synge in stimulating him to complete the two-act version of his play, an ironical situation he must have relished. On 14 September he travelled to Gort and Coole Park where he showed Lady Gregory the completed play and the three sections of *The Aran Islands*. She did not like the play. On 20 September he left for Aran, arriving after one night in Galway. He took his fiddle with him, and feeling no nervousness at the audience in this place, played for the islanders' dancing. While still on Aran he received a letter from Lady Gregory in which she suggested those revisions to *The Aran Islands* already referred to. The Islands were just recovering at this time from a typhus epidemic, and Synge was sufficiently disturbed by what he saw to give his mother a full account when he returned to Dublin on 9 October. The fourth section of *The Aran Islands*, however, only touches lightly on this subject, and is devoted more to the retelling of stories and poems given him by the islanders. It may be that Lady Gregory's advice had not gone altogether unheeded, for while he retained the place-names and precise references she disliked, he did add 'some more faery belief', though none of it had that dreaminess to which she and Yeats were so addicted.

Fourth visit to Aran

He spent October at Crosthwaite Park. Edward Stephens describes him at that time 'sitting with one foot on the mantelpiece and one on the fender . . . as he talked he often spun his folding scissors on his finger, or rolled a cigarette of light tobacco, and I noticed the quick action of his sensitive hands. Sometimes for my amusement when the shoe was off, he would grip the shining steel poker with his toes and put it into the fire. He took a child-like pleasure in this feat.' Synge was, for all his history of sickness and the encroachments of Hodgkin's disease upon his

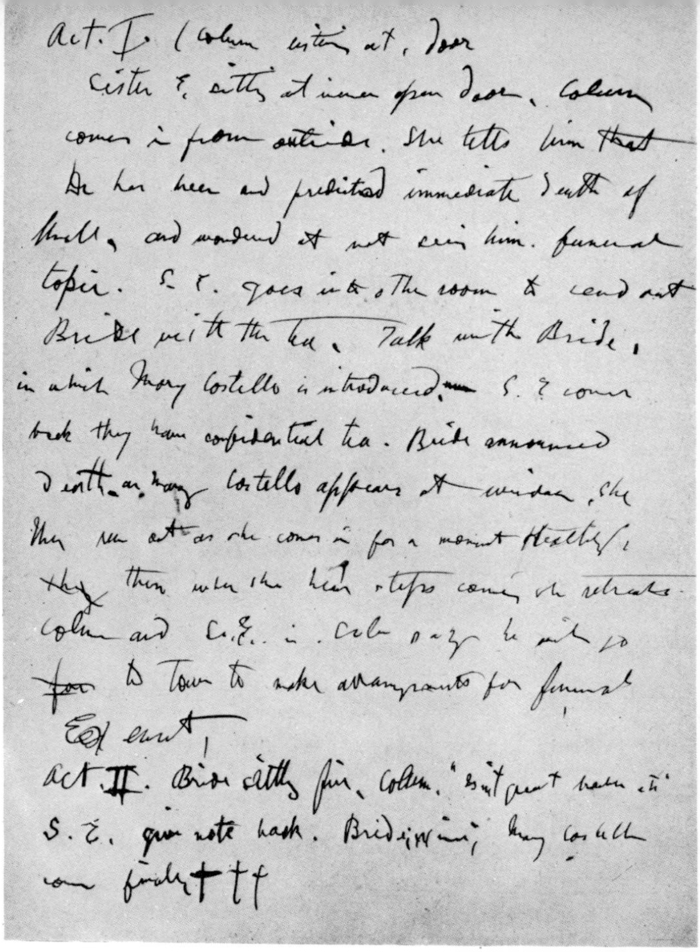

An early draft of *When the Moon Has Set*

vitality, a man who took pleasure in the strength and dexterity of his own body. The previous year on Aran he had entertained and astonished the islanders with various gymnastic tricks, and he was, until his very last illness, always capable of long walks and cycle rides through the most difficult terrain. Jack B. Yeats wrote of him, 'Synge was by nature well equipped for the roads. Though his health was often bad he had beating under his ribs a brave heart that carried him over rough tracks. He gathered about him very little gear, and cared nothing for comfort except perhaps that of a good turf fire. He was, though young in years, "an old dog for a hard road and not a young pup for a tow-path".'

Synge returned to Paris in November, pausing in London to leave the now completed manuscript of *The Aran Islands* with Grant Richards, who rejected it because he thought it lacked general appeal. The year ended, as so many years before it, with frustration.

'The Aran Islands' completed

69

It is hard to determine why it was that 1902 proved to be so extraordinarily creative a year for Synge. He had been impressed by the performance in Gaelic of Douglas Hyde's play, *The Twisting of the Rope*, which had been presented by the Irish Literary Theatre in October 1901 under the direction of Willie Fay, and had thought it more important than Yeats' and Moore's *Diarmuid and Grania* which F.R. Benson's company had performed on the same occasion. He thought that it pointed to a new direction for Irish drama. He had also had the opportunity of more discussions with Lady Gregory at Coole, and it is probable that to her condemnation of *When the Moon Has Set* she had added the rider that he might consider writing peasant drama. Whatever the reasons, it was now that he began the work that was to establish him not merely as a member, but as a leader of the Irish renaissance.

The year began badly, however. Synge had also submitted *The Aran Islands* to Fisher Unwin, and on 21 January he received another notice of its rejection. His mother, writing that month to Samuel, reported the earlier rejection by Grant Richards, and said: 'Poor Johnnie! We could all have told him that, but then men like Yeats and the rest get round him and make him think Irish literature and the Celtic language are very important, and, I am sorry to say, Johnnie seems to believe all they tell him. Now perhaps his eyes are beginning to be opened in that direction. . . .' In fact, Synge was now more earnestly concerned with matters Irish than ever before. He attended regularly Jubainville's twice-weekly classes in Old Irish at the Sorbonne, and in March contributed an article on 'La Vieille Littérature Irlandaise' to *L'Européen*. In May *L'Européen* published a further

Willie Fay

article on 'Le Mouvement Intellectuel Irlandais'. On 7 June *The Speaker* published his review of Lady Gregory's *Cuchulain of Muirthemne*, and on 6 September a review of David Comyn's edition of Geoffrey Keating's *Foras Feasa Ar Eirinn: The History of Ireland*. Keating had, of course, interested him for some time, and in Paris that spring he began work on two verse plays, one of which was based upon Keating's story of Luasnad, Capa and Laighne, the three fishermen who landed in Ireland and were drowned with their wives by the Flood. The other he referred to in his diary as 'Vernal play in verse', and he appears to have worked on both plays at the same time. He was writing the Keating play on 17 March, finishing *A Vernal Play* on 27 March, and was engaged in revising both on 13 April.

Verse plays

Only fragments of these two plays now exist, though the *Luasnad, Capa and Laine* (Synge's spelling) fragments, as edited by Dr Saddlemyer, do form a coherent whole. The plays are in such marked contrast to each other that it is impossible not to believe that they were intended to be complementary. *A Vernal Play* is set in a Wicklow glen. It is a 'soft kind morning on the hills' and two girls, Etain and Niave, are out picking wild flowers when they meet Cermuid and his wife Boinn. After some conversation filled with the mood of pastoral peace they are met by an Old Man who calls himself 'friend of love', and says:

> I think bad of men dying and death bends
> When men make talk of love.

The play breaks off shortly after this, and the next fragment reveals that the Old Man has died. Etain, Boinn and Niave 'rhyme and death rhyme' over him, but the fragment ends with a reassertion of love and joy in the natural world.

Luasnad, Capa and Laine on the other hand is set on a bleak mountain as yet uncovered by the rising flood. Every hope of escape or delivery is destroyed as soon as voiced. Luasnad's wife gives birth to a child.

> LAINE: Your child is born, Luasnad, and it lives.
> CAPA: It is the first man's child has cried on Banba.
> LUASNAD: It will be the first dead human body.

Soon only Luasnad and Laine's wife are left alive. Luasnad has already said:

> All this life has been a hurtful game
> Played out by steps of anguish. Every beast
> Is bred with fearful torment in the womb
> And bred by fearful torments in life-blood.
> Yet by a bait of love the aimless gods
> Have made us multitudes.

Now, alone with Laine's widow, and as a last gesture of defiance, a last assertion that Man's high mood

> Can pass above this passion of the seas
> That moans to crush him,

he tells her he loves her, and they make love before they are swept away to their deaths.

In both plays love is seen as the answer to the fear of death. In *A Vernal Play* the statement is made gently, lyrically, and in *Luasnad, Capa and Laine*, harshly, dramatically. The former clearly owes much to Synge's knowledge of the Wicklow glens and the latter owes a great deal to his observation of the barren savagery of the Aran landscape. The end of *A Vernal Play* has some similarities to the end of Yeats' *Shadowy Waters* which Synge had read, and *Luasnad, Capa and Laine* has speeches reminiscent of *King Lear* which had been the third production of the Irish Literary Theatre in the previous October. Synge was still using literature as his inspiration.

When he returned to Ireland that summer he turned to personal experience rather than literature for his material, and in a burst of astounding creative energy began and completed both *Riders to the Sea* and *In the Shadow of the Glen*. The two plays again appear to have been written over the same period, and again form a contrast. *Riders to the Sea* is, like *Luasnad, Capa and Laine*, a tragic and even epic play, set in a bare Aran landscape threatened by the sea. *In the Shadow of the Glen*, while hardly being as romantically pastoral as *A Vernal Play*, is set in Wicklow and, by means of the tramp's speeches, asserts the joy of the natural world as vividly as *Riders to the Sea* asserts the inevitability of solitude and death.

It seems as if in his two pairs of plays Synge was presenting two of his own dominant feelings, that of despair, frustration and bitterness, and that of sympathy with all that was most passionate, free, wild and amorous. The clashes of the passionate heart with the rigorous intelligence, of the impulse towards love and beauty with the narrow morality of convention, of the small human individual with the forces of mortality: these were his central dramatic conflicts at this time.

The plays were written at Tomrilands House in Wicklow, where the family had their usual summer holiday, though this year there is no record of there being any visiting ladies. There is every indication, however, that Synge spent much time wandering the hills and glens and talking to the country folk. He also worked on prose essays, and reviewed Seamus MacManus' *Donegal Fairy Stories* for *The Speaker* of 21 June. In his review he said of MacManus' style, after quoting a sample passage: 'Such a style has a certain liveliness, yet when it is chosen by Irish writers a great deal of what is most precious in the national life must be omitted

'Riders to the Sea'
and
'In the Shadow of the Glen'
completed

A cabin in Wicklow. It is in such a place, 'the last cottage at the head of a long glen', that *In the Shadow of the Glen* is set. In that play Nora cries, '. . . what good is a bit of a farm with cows on it, and sheep on the back hills, when you do be sitting, looking out from a door the like of that door, and seeing nothing but the mists rolling down the bog, and the mists again, and they rolling up the bog, and hearing nothing but the wind crying out in the bits of broken trees that were left from the great storm, and the streams roaring with the rain?'

from their work, or imperfectly expressed. On the other hand the rollicking note is present in the Irish character – present to an extent some writers of the day do not seem to be aware of – and it demands, if we choose to deal with it, a free rollicking style.' It appears to have been about the time that this review was published that

Synge started work on his third significant play, *The Tinker's Wedding*, in which that 'rollicking note' is present.

For Synge there was little gap between his critical theory and his creative practice. His articles and reviews point always to concerns which were animating his imagination of the time. Thus, his essay on 'The Old and New in Ireland' which was published in September gives us a clear picture of his attitude towards the revival of the Gaelic language and towards the language of his own drama. One passage also supports the view that he was, in his plays of that year, deliberately concerned with contrasting moods. After commenting upon the previous dearth of valuable *On Irish* books of Irish literature, he wrote: 'Now everything is changed. We have fine *literature* editions of books by W. B. Yeats and other Irish writers in all our bookshop windows. One evening we can read *The Shadowy Waters* and catch a tenuous sadness, such as we find in Aglavaine et Selysette, and the next evening we can go on to some new writer in the Irish language, and read some little work like *Faith and Famine*, by Father Dineen, where we have vigour and talent, using a form and psychology that recall the predecessors of Titus Andronicus or Tamburlaine.' If Father Dineen had read those crude predecessors he cannot have been much gratified by Synge's comment, but Synge himself must have recognized his own use of 'tenuous sadness' in *A Vernal Play*, and of Marlovian vigour in *Luasnad, Capa and Laine*.

In the next paragraph of his article he wrote: 'This double way in which the new Irish spirit is showing itself has many points of interest. With the present generation the linguistic atmosphere of Ireland has become definitely English enough, for the first time, to allow work to be done in English that is perfectly Irish in its essence, yet has sureness and purity of form.' Later he expressed a fear that the Gaelic League's effort to revive Irish might 'stifle the English once more', and spoke of the advantages that had been derived from 'the final decay of Irish among the national classes of Leinster'. He suggested that 'If . . . the Gaelic League can keep the cruder powers of the Irish mind occupied in a healthy and national way till the influence of Irish literature, written in English, is more definite in Irish life, the half-cultured classes may come over to the side of the others, and give an intellectual unity to the country of the highest value.'

On Lady Gregory It is a view which must have irritated a large number of Irish Nationalists, but it is one which he held throughout his life. In Lady Gregory's *Cuchullain of Muirthemne* which he also reviewed that summer he found a 'wonderfully simple and powerful language that resembles a good deal the peasant dialect of the west of Ireland'. He added: 'The peasants of the west of Ireland speak an almost Elizabethan dialect, and in the lyrical episodes it is often hard to say when Lady Gregory is thinking of the talk of the peasants and when she is thinking of some passage

I've a cramp in my)

back,and my hip's asleep on me,there's been the devil's own
fly iching my nose...It's near dead I was and you blathering
about the rain and Darcy --(<u>bitterly</u>)--the devil choke him,
and the towering church.--(<u>crying out impatiently</u>)--Give me that
whiskey.Would you have herself come back before I taste a drop
at all.

(<u>Tramp gives him the glass</u>)--

Dan.<u>(after drinking)</u> Go over now ~~and open~~ *to* that cupboard,stranger,
~~too open the door.~~ *and bring me a black stick*
~~Tramp.Is it your old clothes that you want?~~ *you'll see)*
~~Dan.What is it you see~~ in the west corner by the wall&
~~Tramp.A bit of a black stick,master of the house.~~
~~Dan.Bring that stick,stranger.~~

~~(~~Tramp brings it over)--*Is it that, master of the house ?*

Dan.(<u>taking it</u>) It's a long while I'm keeping that stick,
~~stranger~~ for I've a bad wife in the house, ~~for the~~ *stranger*
~~Tramp. is it the woman went out?~~

~~Dan. it is stranger,And it is a bad wife she is~~ a bad wife for an
old man,and ~~I'm~~ *it's* getting old, *I am)* God help me,though ~~I've~~ I've an
arm to me still.--(<u>he shakes the stick</u>)--Wait ~~a little~~ *(while)* stranger, *you* *now)*
and it's a great sight you'll see in this room,in two hours or
three,a great sight surely...(<u>he stops to listen</u>)--~~Is that~~

A page from the typescript of *In the Shadow of the Glen*

in the Old Testament. In several chapters, again, there are pages where battles and chariot/fights are described with a nearly Eastern prolixity, in a rich tone that has the cadence of the palace, and not the cadence of men who are poor. This union of notes, fugitive as it is, forms perhaps the most interesting feature of the language of the book. The Elizabethan vocabulary has a force and colour that make it the only form of English that is quite suitable for incidents of the epic kind, and in her intercourse with the peasants of the west Lady Gregory has learned to use this vocabulary in a new way, while she carries with her plaintive Gaelic constructions that make her language, in a true sense, a language of Ireland.'

He referred in his review to 'a few other writers' who 'have been moving gradu/ ally towards' this particular cadence and it is clear that he numbered himself among them. His two reviews were, indeed, statements of his own beliefs about the language he was using at that time to write *Riders to the Sea* and *In the Shadow of the Glen*.

Fifth visit to Aran

On 8 October 1902 he arrived at Coole with the finished manuscripts of both plays, and then went onwards to Aran where he stayed on Inisheer at Michael Costello's public house. He returned to Dublin on 9 November and on 4 Decem/ ber saw the Fay brothers again present *The Twisting of the Rope*. It was badly attended and the stage was too small. As the year ended Synge decided to go to London and there seek publication for his Aran book and his plays. He had already begun *The Tinker's Wedding* and was now completely assured of his role in Irish letters. He had found his language and had publicly identified it for others, and he had escaped at last from writing as personal therapy to writing as art.

Stephen MacKenna (left) with William Gibson (centre), President of the Gaelic League

John Masefield

Arthur Symons

Until he arrived in London on 9 January 1903 Synge had met relatively few other writers and artists. While he was very much a part of the W.B. Yeats-Lady Gregory circle in Ireland, his only other literary friends were Richard Best and Stephen MacKenna. Now, however, once he had settled into his boarding-house at 4 Handel Street, Brunswick Square, he found himself reading his plays aloud to literary gatherings both in Lady Gregory's rooms and those of Yeats, and becoming acquainted with Arthur Symons, G. K. Chesterton, John Masefield and others. Masefield he particularly liked, and they became close enough friends for Synge to show him some of his poems long before he admitted to Yeats that he was still writing verse. He also made the rounds of the editors, and on 18 April, J. L. Hammond, the new editor of *The Speaker*, published his review of Pierre Loti's *L'Inde (sans les Anglais)*, J. K. Huysman's *L'Oblat* and Anatole France's *Monsieur Bergeret à Paris*. Arthur Symons asked to see *Riders to the Sea* for the *Fortnightly Review* but did not accept it. R. Brimley Johnson, the publisher, also

London and
literary friends

77

asked to read it but with the same result. John Masefield busied himself with trying to interest Elkin Mathews in *The Aran Islands*. Though nothing much seemed to be coming of all these efforts Synge felt sufficiently encouraged by the interest his work had aroused to go over to France on 6 March to move his effects from the rue d'Assas, and give up his connection with Paris. In Paris he spent a good deal of time with James Joyce, who at first disliked *Riders to the Sea*, but later admired it enough to translate it into Italian. He did not see Thérèse Beydon. Margaret Hardon was back in America, getting married. Hope Rea was in London, though there is no diary entry to suggest that he saw her there.

Synge abandons Paris

Synge returned to London on 13 March and got back to Dublin five days later in time to see the Fay brothers, who had now formed their own company, performing Yeats' *The Hour Glass* and Lady Gregory's *Twenty-Five*, her first play, in the Molesworth Hall. Following the success of the Fays' earlier production of AE's *Deirdre* and Yeats' *Cathleen ni Houlihan* in April 1902, Yeats, Maud Gonne

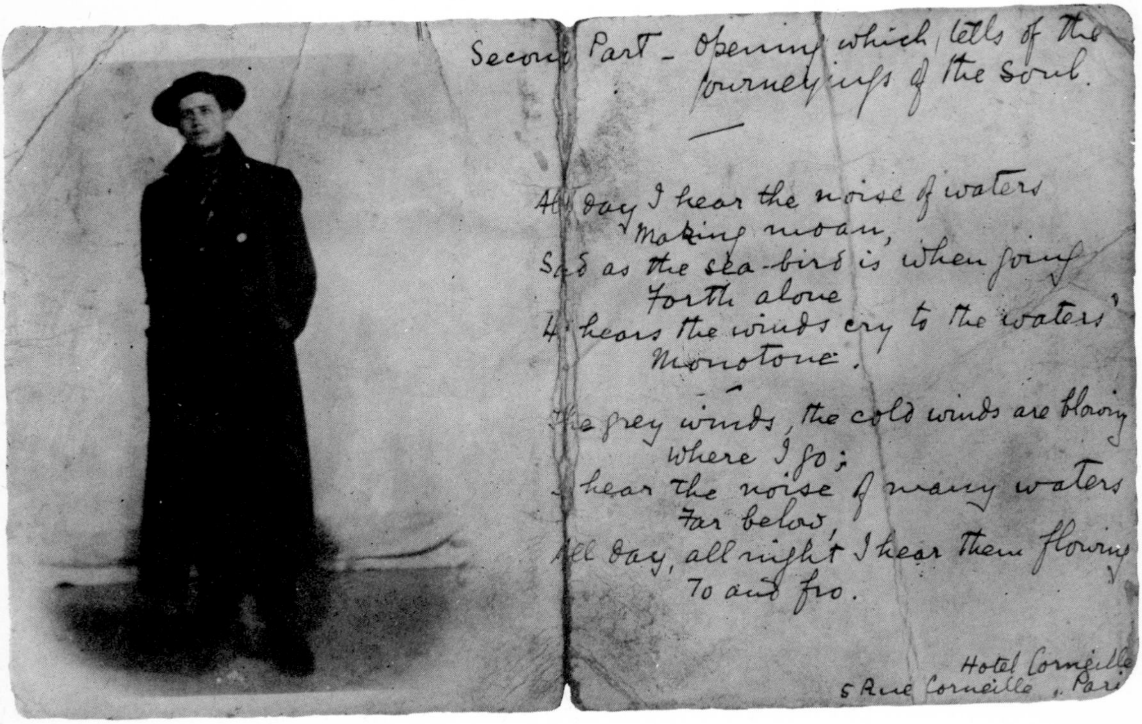

James Joyce's postcard from the Hotel Corneille in Paris, 1895. Both Joyce and Synge used the Hotel Corneille, but they did not get to know each other well until 1903

and Douglas Hyde had founded the Irish National Theatre Society, and the Fays' company, entirely professional by this time, was at the heart of the movement. In May they took Yeats' *The Hour Glass, Cathleen ni Houlihan* and *The Pot of Broth,* Lady Gregory's *Twenty-Five* and Fred Ryan's *The Laying of the Foundations* to the Queens Gate Hall, Kensington, and had a rousing success. It must have been with high hopes, therefore, that Synge sat with the company in Lady Gregory's rooms in Nassau Street, Dublin that June, and heard her read *In the Shadow of the Glen.* He sat at the back of the room, and when he spoke, spoke quietly. He seemed almost austere. The actors were impressed, even startled by the play's novelty and harsh vigour. The Fays decided to produce it in the autumn.

Synge did not go to Tomrilands House with his mother that summer, but, armed with an address his brother Robert had given him, went instead to West Kerry, and stayed in the hill-top cottage of Philly Harris, at Mountain Stage near Glenbeigh. Here he listened to the many stories of Philly and his brother Denis,

First visit to West Kerry

Douglas Hyde (standing), a founder, with Yeats and Maude Gonne, of the Irish National Theatre Society

The Irish National Theatre Society.

President : W. B. YEATS.

Vice-Presidents :
DOUGLAS HYDE and GEORGE RUSSELL.

Stage Manager : W. G. FAY. Secretary : F. M. RYAN.

PROGRAMME.

Molesworth Hall, Molesworth Street,

DUBLIN,

THURSDAY, FRIDAY & SATURDAY EVENINGS,

8th, 9th & 10th October, 1903, at 8.15.

Prices of Admission : 3s., 2s., & 1s.

An Cló-Cumann (Teóranta), Clódóirí Gaedilge, áe Cliat

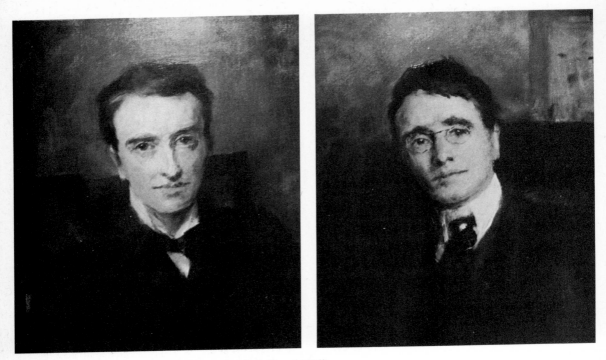

The Fay brothers, Frank (left) and Willie

became familiar with the local tramps who made the cottage a regular port of call, and filled notebook upon notebook with anecdotes and examples of the colourful speech of the people. It was in Kerry that he found the vivid language he used later in *The Playboy of the Western World*, and many of the most entertaining and inventive speeches in that play are taken almost direct from the mouths of the Kerry folk, who were bilingual to a degree unknown in Aran, and whose natural mode of English speech was more harshly poetical and figurative than any Synge had yet heard. He was now working on *The Tinker's Wedding*. He returned to Dublin on 19 September to find that the Fays were rehearsing *In the Shadow of the Glen* together with Yeats' *The King's Threshold* and *Cathleen ni Houlihan*. The Fays felt that *Riders to the Sea* needed further revision before production. Yeats, however, published it that month in *Samhain*, the magazine he had founded to support and publicize the Irish Literary Theatre, alongside Douglas Hyde's *The Twisting of the Rope* in its original Gaelic and in an English translation. The *Manchester Guardian* reviewed the issue, and described *Riders to the Sea* as 'the most poignant piece of tragic drama that we have seen written in English since Mr Phillips' *Paolo and*

'Riders to the Sea' published

Maire ni Shiublaigh (Maire Walker) who played Nora Burke in the first production of *In the Shadow of the Glen*

Francesca'. John Masefield wrote to Synge on 18 December asking for fair copies of both plays as he was determined to interest Elkin Mathews in them.

While *Riders to the Sea* was slowly making its way towards production and publication, the rehearsals of *In the Shadow of the Glen* were causing disquiet. Dudley Digges, a leading actor in the company, refused to play in it and resigned, taking the actress Maire Quinn with him. On the day of the first performance, 8 October, the *Irish Independent* stated that Mr Synge, who 'lives his life between the gaiety of Paris and the homes of the fisher folk on the Aran Islands . . . did not

First performance of 'In the Shadow of the Glen'

81

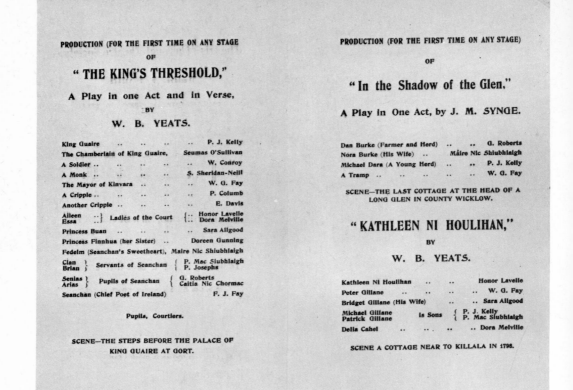

Programme for the first production of *In the Shadow of the Glen*, in October 1903

Criticism derive his inspiration from the Western Isles,' and suggested that those who wished for a 'pure and National' dramatic art should raise their voices against this 'perversion' of the aims of the Irish National Theatre Society. It was mainly the plot which disturbed them. The thought that an Irish husband could pretend to be dead in order to catch his wife with her lover, and then throw her out after the lover had rejected her was bad enough, but the notion that any Irish woman, however miserably married, would commit adultery was anathema. The first performance was hissed. The *Irish Times* detected a 'slur on Irish womanhood'. The *United Irishman*, which had earlier published an article by John Butler Yeats praising the play for its attack upon 'our Irish institution, the loveless marriage', said that the

82

Willie Fay as the Tramp, and Maire ni Shiublaigh as Nora, in *In the Shadow of the Glen*

J. M. Synge in April 1905, a drawing by John Butler Yeats

play was 'a corrupt version of that old world libel on womankind, – the "Widow of Ephesus"' and considered Synge 'utterly a stranger to the Irish Character'. W. B. Yeats retorted with a letter attacking the ignorance and narrow-mindedness of Gaelic propagandists, Nationalist zealots and philistine priests. Arthur Griffith counterpunched with the assertion that Irishwomen were the most virtuous on earth. James Connolly supported Griffith, maintaining that 'At present we need a National Theatre, not for the purpose of enlarging our national vanity, but of restoring our proper national pride.' Even Maud Gonne wrote of 'writers who permit foreign thoughts and philosophies to creep in and distort their heroes and heroines'. John Butler Yeats returned to the fray in the *United Irishman* on 31 October and repeated his view that 'it is a very effective attack on loveless marriages – the most miserable institution so dear to our thrifty elders among the peasants and among their betters, by whom anything like impulse or passion is discredited, human nature coerced at every point and sincerity banished from the land.' He added: 'My complaint of Mr Synge's play is that it did not go far enough.' Griffith commented that the elder Yeats spent most of his life outside Ireland and was ignorant of the Irish character.

Arthur Griffith

Synge himself remained quiet during the debate. He did, however, draft, either then or on the renewal of the controversy after the 1905 production, *National Drama: A Farce*, in which he mocked the foolishness of 'wilful nationalism' that demanded a drama that should display 'the virtue of its country' without 'the plague spot of sex'; and he allowed Fogarty, his own spokesman, to suggest that all good art is national because it used the 'infinite number of influences' of the country of its origin to produce 'a local character which is all a nation can demand'.

Objections did not come only from the wilful Nationalists, however. Stephen MacKenna said he preferred an 'ideal breezy-spring-dayish Cuchullainoid etc. National Theatre', and added 'Modern Problems even in peasant robes I do not like to see made public property in Ireland yet.' Synge replied at length saying, 'Heaven forbid that we should have a morbid sex-obseded [*sic*] drama in Ireland, not because we have any peculiar sanctity which I utterly deny – blessed unripeness is sometimes akin to damned rottenness, see percentage of lunatics in Ireland and causes thereof – but because it is bad as drama and is played out. On [the] French stage you get sex without its balancing elements: on [the] Irish stage you get [the] other elements without sex. I restored sex and the people were so surprised they saw the sex only. . . .' He added in a postscript, 'I have as you know perambulated a good deal of Ireland in my [thirty] years and if I were [to] tell, which Heaven forbid, all the sex-horrors I have seen I could a tale unfold that would wither up your blood. . . . I think squeamishness is a disease, and that Ireland will gain if writers deal manfully, directly and *decently* with the entire reality of life. . . .'

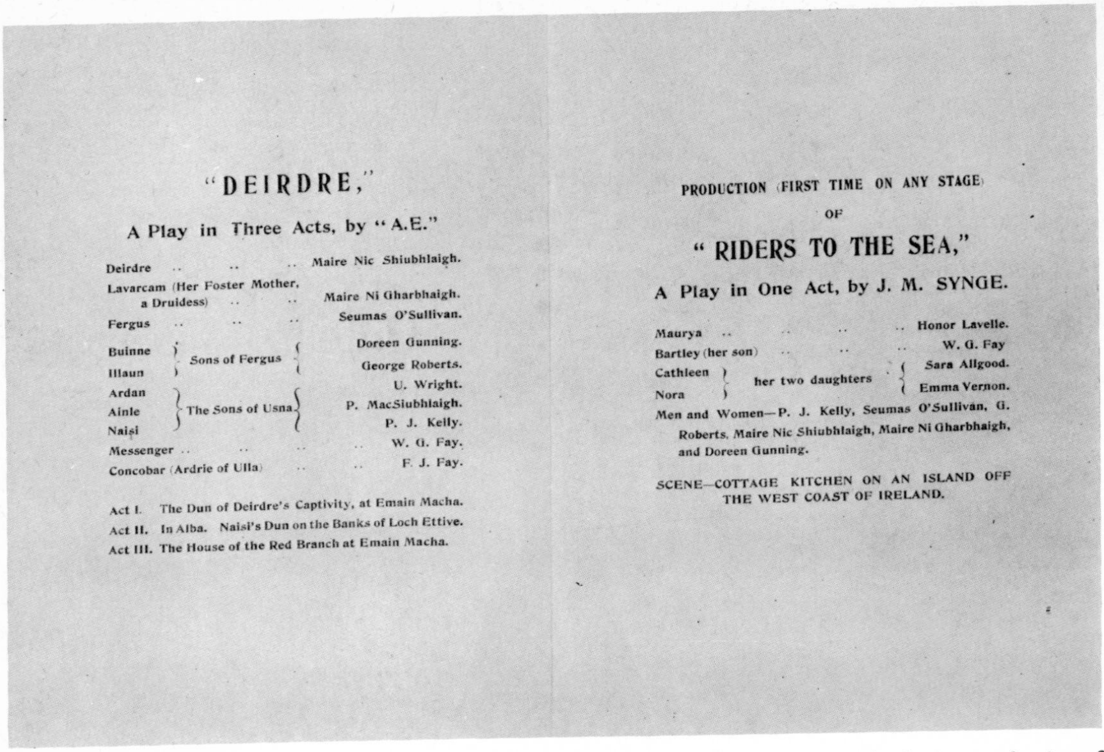

"DEIRDRE,"

A Play in Three Acts, by "A.E."

Deirdre		Maire Nic Shiubhlaigh.
Lavarcam (Her Foster Mother, a Druidess)		Maire Ni Gharbhaigh.
Fergus		Seumas O'Sullivan.
Buinne	Sons of Fergus	Doreen Gunning.
Illaun		George Roberts.
Ardan	The Sons of Usna	U. Wright.
Ainle		P. MacSiubhlaigh.
Naisi		P. J. Kelly.
Messenger		W. G. Fay.
Concobar (Ardrie of Ulla)		F. J. Fay.

Act I. The Dun of Deirdre's Captivity, at Emain Macha.
Act II. In Alba. Naisi's Dun on the Banks of Loch Ettive.
Act III. The House of the Red Branch at Emain Macha.

PRODUCTION (FIRST TIME ON ANY STAGE)
OF
"RIDERS TO THE SEA,"

A Play in One Act, by J. M. SYNGE.

Maurya		Honor Lavelle.
Bartley (her son)		W. G. Fay
Cathleen	her two daughters	Sara Allgood.
Nora		Emma Vernon.

Men and Women—P. J. Kelly, Seumas O'Sullivan, G. Roberts, Maire Nic Shiubhlaigh, Maire Ni Gharbhaigh, and Doreen Gunning.

SCENE—COTTAGE KITCHEN ON AN ISLAND OFF THE WEST COAST OF IRELAND.

Irish National Theatre Society programme for the first production of *Riders to the Sea*

First performance of 'Riders to the Sea'

It may have been the strain of this controversy that helped to make the cold Synge contracted in November debilitating enough to send him to bed, where, still conscious of the swollen gland in his neck, he feared tuberculosis. He had recovered by the end of the year, however, and on 25 February 1904 *Riders to the Sea* had its first performance, together with AE's *Deirdre*. Even Griffith's *United Irishman* grudgingly admitted its 'Tragic beauty', though, with that squeamishness Synge detested, it objected to the presence of a coffin on stage. Synge himself took part in the direction and got samples of cloth from Aran and some pairs of pampooties so that it might be dressed correctly. On 26 March 1904 Synge's two plays were presented in London together with *The King's Threshold* at the Royalty Theatre, and *Riders to the Sea* was greatly praised while *In the Shadow of the Glen* was largely ignored. Meanwhile Synge himself, in Dublin, was working on a two-act version of *The Tinker's Wedding*, now called *The Movements of May*, and completing *The Well of the Saints*. Again it seems that he was working on two plays at once, arranging to present two complementary treatments of a theme. In

Brigit O'Dempsey,
Sara Allgood, and Maire
O'Neill in the 1906
production of *Riders to the Sea*

each play the Christian viewpoint is challenged and conquered by the viewpoint of the vagrant. In *The Tinker's Wedding* Sara Casey is young, filled with a sense of her own beauty; in *The Well of the Saints* Mary Doul, no less assured of her own attractions, is old. In both cases the representative of Christianity fails to understand the situation. The one play ends in farce and riot after much savagery and wildness and the other in something approaching the stoic and tragic.

While Synge was working, the Irish Literary Theatre was in the throes of getting itself a permanent theatre. Annie Horniman, a theosophist friend of Yeats, was putting up the money and generally acting as fairy godmother. After handing *The Well of the Saints* to Willie Fay on 16 July, Synge visited Coole and there the whole business was discussed with AE and Yeats. The negotiations were complex and arduous, but in spite of one barrister asking if the Irish National Theatre Society had ever produced a play which was an attack on the institution of marriage, the patent was granted, and on 20 August 1904 the Abbey Theatre was born.

*Birth of
the Abbey Theatre*

ABBEY THEATRE,
Lower Abbey St. and Marlborough St.

THE IRISH NATIONAL THEATRE SOCIETY will give the Opening Performances of the Season on Tuesday 27th, Wednesday 28th, Thursday 29th, Friday 30th, and Saturday 31st December, 1904, and on Monday 2nd, and Tuesday 3rd, January, 1905, at 8.15 p.m.

ON BAILE'S STRAND, by W. B. Yeats, and **SPREADING THE NEWS,** by Lady Gregory, will be produced every evening. In addition to these two Plays, **KATHLEEN NI HOULIHAN,** by W. B. Yeats, and **IN THE SHADOW OF THE GLEN,** by J. M. Synge, will be played alternately.

Seats can be Booked at Cramer, Wood & Co's., Westmoreland Street, after 14th December. Stalls 3s.; Balcony 2s.

Un petit groupe de jeunes irlandais et irlandaises se sont décidés à donner une orientation dramatique au mouvement littéraire auquel ils appartiennent et qui porte le titre de " Renaissance celtique." Ces jeunes gens qui sont, à ce que l'on m'a dit, employés dans les maisons de commerce de Dublin pendant la journée, consacrent leurs soirées à jouer des pièces du poète W. B. Yeats, de Lady Gregory et d'autres personnalités de l'Ecole celtique. Ces acteurs manquent naturellement d'habileté, mais ils ont l'enthousiasme et la foi qui valent mieux qu'elle. Ce " théâtre national irlandais " qu'ils ont fondé dans un sincère élan patriotique a pour résultat une réelle purification de l'art théâtral. La mise en scène est réduite à son minimum, les jeux de scène conventionnels sont bannis ou plutôt inconnus, une simplicité frugale caractérise toute l'entreprise, bref c'est aussi un art plein de soupirs.

Les petites pièces qu'ils jouent ont trait à la vie fruste des paysans irlandais, à leur fatalisme, à leur résignation, à leur tendance au rêve. Leurs émotions restent contenues, leurs amours sont chastes, ils ont la calme dignité de ceux qui ont renoncé. Tout le jeu des acteurs est lui-même en mineur. Ils se remuent mollement et parlent lentement, comme des personnages de rêve ou comme des " pupazzi " malades de Mæterlinck.

En les écoutant, vous vous sentez envahis par une suave et douce mélancolie J'ajoute que lorsqu'ils chantent les vers libres de M. Yeats où qu'ils murmurent sa prose harmonieuse, leur prononciation de notre langue est un délice pour toute oreille anglaise. L'impression d'ensemble est d'un haut romantisme. N'a-t on pas déjà défini le romantisme comme un mélange de beauté et d'étrangeté. Certainement la beauté de ces représentations irlandaises est étrange, étranche et fraîche, étrange et troublante.

C'est une chose étonnante que de voir l'art antique, épuisé, du théâtre se renouveler ou plutôt naître à nouveau dans le cœur de ce petit peuple irlandais.—A. B. WALKLEY, in " Le Temps."

One great charm of the Irish performances lay in the judgment with which the two programmes were composed. What could be more delightful than a " triple bill " of this sort ?—a majestic opening, to exalt the imagination ; a pathetic sequel, to touch the heart ; a comic finale to relieve the nervous tension, and send the audience away refreshed and exhilarated. . . . . Every one of these plays was listened to with real pleasure, and all were heartily applauded. A more frank and authentic success the Irish Company could not have desired. . . . . Our warmest admiration and respect are justly due to the enthusiasm which animates these young artists, and the dignity and sincerity of all their work.—WILLIAM ARCHER, in the " World," March 29th, 1904.

The afternoon's programme included three little plays : One by Mr. Yeats, " The King's Threshold," and two by Mr. J. M. Synge, " Riders to the Sea " and " In the Shadow of the Glen." Very widely though the three plays differed from one another, from all one derived the same quality of pleasure—the pleasure in something quite simple and quite strange. There was in none of the plays any structural complexity, and yet none of them was not truly dramatic . . . . Certainly the Irish Theatre was an Oasis.—MAX BEERBOHM, in the "Saturday Review," 9th April, 1904.

The Irish National Theatre Society, who gave two performances at the Royalty Theatre last week . . . is perhaps the most characteristic expression of a very notable renaissance in the literary and artistic expression of imaginative thought, which has been growing in Ireland in these later years.—P.C. in " Vanity Fair," April 7th, 1904.

Sealy, Bryer, & Walker, Dublin. 4544-12-04

An Abbey Theatre announcement of 1904

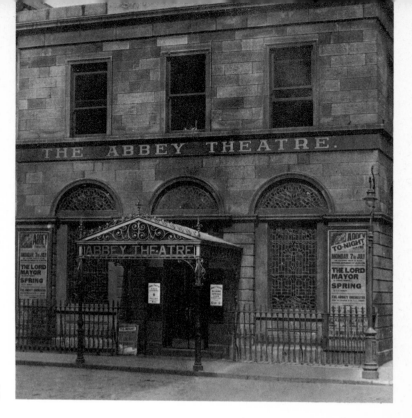

The old Abbey Theatre, Dublin,
an early photograph

Synge was not present at the birth. He left for Philly Harris' Kerry cottage at the beginning of August. There Yeats wrote to him suggesting that the phrase 'God Almighty' was used a little too frequently in *The Well of the Saints* and commenting that one phrase reminded him a little too closely of *King Lear*. Synge returned to Dublin at the end of August and then, on 17 September, went off to Mayo for the first time, staying in Sligo for a few days and then, after going to Belmullet by boat, cycling. 'In Mayo,' he wrote in his notebook, 'one cannot forget that in spite of the beauty of the landscape the people in it are debased and nearly demoralized by bad housing and lodging and the endless misery of the rain.' On his return he felt, as he told MacKenna, 'lonesome and uncanny', and rather than live in Crosthwaite Park which had become crowded because of the return of Samuel and his family from China and the visit of his cousin Stewart Ross and his child, on 10 October he took a room at 15 Maxwell Road, Rathmines.

In Kerry
and Mayo

In December Masefield offered Synge the opportunity to write for the *Manchester Guardian*, and two essays, 'An Impression of Aran' and 'The Oppression of the Hills' were published in early 1905. In December 1904 the Abbey Theatre opened its doors, and Yeats published *In the Shadow of the Glen* in *Samhain*. John

'In the Shadow
of the Glen'
published

89

Quinn, the American lawyer, published an edition of fifty copies in New York at the same time. Mrs Synge viewed the patronage of Miss Horniman with astonishment. 'She must be a little mad,' she commented.

Willie Fay still had some reservations about *The Well of the Saints*, finding some parts of it not true to the Irish character. Synge responded firmly: 'What I write of Irish country life I know to be true, and I most emphatically will not change a syllable of it because A, B or C think they know better than I do.' At this time, shortly before the production of *The Well of the Saints*, Arthur Griffith renewed his attack on *In the Shadow of the Glen* and for a while the precise origin of the plot was debated publicly. Synge himself joined in with a temperate letter explaining that he had got the story from Pat Dirane. The controversy acted as an overture to the production of *The Well of the Saints* on 4 February which was ill received and attacked on the grounds of its un-Irishness. The *Freeman's Journal* felt that 'the point of view is not that of a writer in sympathetic touch with the people from whom

First performance of 'The Well of the Saints'

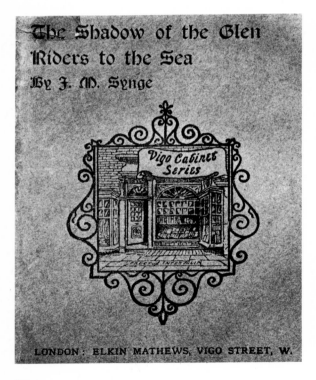

The cover of Synge's first book, published by Elkin Mathews in 1905, in his Vigo Cabinet series

Molly Allgood

he purports to draw his characters'. Arthur Griffith suggested that the language was less Irish than Whitechapel cockney, a curious critical judgement. Synge did not contribute further to the controversy. On 15 February 1905 he left his Rathmines lodging and returned to Crosthwaite Park. Although *The Well of the Saints* had not brought Synge much popularity, it had brought him something else. Molly Allgood, the nineteen-year-old sister of Sarah Allgood, one of the company's leading actresses, had recently left her work as a shopgirl and joined the Fay company, and she had been given a walk-on part in the play. Synge was soon to fall in love with her. *Molly Allgood*

Meanwhile, however, Elkin Mathews had at last decided to bring out *Riders to the Sea* and *In the Shadow of the Glen* as a volume of his Vigo Cabinet series. He asked Synge also about *The Tinker's Wedding*, but Synge told him that, being in two acts, it would, if added to the others, make the book too long and, in any case was 'likely to displease a good many of our Dublin friends'. The contract was signed on 22 March 1905. Elkin Mathews had the right to publish the plays for seven years; Synge was to receive a ten per cent royalty. Even as the contract was being signed, however, *Riders to the Sea* received its second printing alongside Douglas Hyde's *The Twisting of the Rope* in the March 1905 issue of *Poet Lore* (Boston) under the inaccurate heading *Two Plays from the Gaelic Originals*.

In April, Hugh Lane commissioned John Butler Yeats to make a portrait of Synge for the Dublin Municipal Gallery that he was planning, and European interest in Synge was revealed by Max Meyerfeld asking permission to translate *The Well of the Saints* into German (produced as *Der Heilige Brunnen*, 12 January

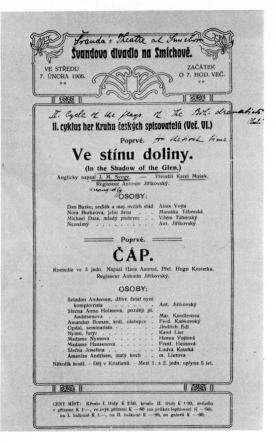

Frouda's Theatre at Smíchov

Švandovo divadlo na Smíchově.

VE STŘEDU
7. ÚNORA 1906.

ZAČÁTEK
O 7. HOD. VEČ.

II. Cycle of the plays of the Brit. dramatists

II. cyklus her Kruhu českých spisovatelů (Več. VI.)

Poprvé. *on different time*

Ve stínu doliny.

(In the Shadow of the Glen.)

Anglicky napsal J. M. Synge. — Přeložil Karel Mušek.
Regisseur Antonín Jiříkovský.
arranged by

OSOBY:

Dan Burke, sedlák a maj. ovčích stád . . Alois Vojta
Nora Burkeova, jeho žena . . . Maruška Táborská
Michael Dara, mladý pastevec . . Vilém Táborský
Neznámý . . . . Ant. Jiříkovský

Poprvé.

ČÁP.

Komedie ve 3 jedn. Napsal Hans Aanrud. Přel. Hugo Kosterka.
Regisseur Antonín Jiříkovský.

OSOBY:

Seladon Andersen, dříve četař nyní
komptoirista . . . . Ant. Jiříkovský
Slečna Anna Holmova, později pí.
Andrisenova . . . . Mar. Kandlerova
Amandus Boman, král. zástupce . Ferd. Kaňkovský
Opdal, seminarista . . . . . . Jindřich Edl
Nymo, furýr . . . . Karel Lier
Madame Nymova . . . . Hanna Vojtová
Madame Hansenova . . . . . . Frant. Hessová
Slečna Josefina . . . . Ludva Kaucká
Amanias Andrisen, malý hoch . . m. Lierová

Několik hostí. - Děj v Kristianii. - Mezi 1. a 2. jedn. uplyne 5 let.

CENY MÍST: Křeslo I. třídy K 2·50, křeslo II. třídy K 1·20, sedadlo
v přízemí K 1·—, ve vyš. přízemí K —·80 (na průkaz legitimaci K —·50),
na I. balkoně K 1·—, na II. balkoně K —·80, na galerii K —·60.

Programme of the first
production of the Czech
translation of *In the Shadow of
the Glen*, 1905

1906), and Karel Mušek seeking to translate *In the Shadow of the Glen* into Czech (produced as *Ve stínu doliny* in Prague, 7 February 1906). The following month, Robert Synge took his brother on a fishing holiday in Donegal from 4 to 11 May, staying at a small hotel at Milford and cycling all over the area. On their return C. P. Scott of the *Manchester Guardian* commissioned Synge to visit the 'Congested Districts' with Jack Yeats and write a series of articles about them with Jack Yeats' illustrations. They set out on 3 June 1905 and covered large areas of Connemara and Mayo. The Congested Districts consisted of the poverty-stricken and infertile lands of the West, and were so called because they were broken up into small and uneconomical holdings that were unable to support their owners or tenants. The Congested Districts Board had been founded in 1891 as a consequence of Land Agitation to establish industries wherever possible, to enlarge

Donegal

*Connemara and
Mayo*

C.P. Scott

Jack B. Yeats

small-holdings by breaking up large estates or by other means, to improve communications, and to fight poverty and starvation. Synge wrote of the poverty and suffering with restraint, and of the peasantry with admiration. Only towards the end of his series did he betray his distrust of the easy solutions of bureaucracy and his hatred of the corruption and nepotism which added to the problems of the people.

After he got back to Dublin and had collected a miserable £25. 4s. 0d., which was less than Jack Yeats got, and caused him to refer to the *Guardian* collectively as 'dirty skunks', he wrote to Stephen MacKenna, '... we had a wonderful journey, and as we had a purse to pull on we pushed into out-of-the-way corners in Mayo and Galway that were more strange and marvellous than anything I've dreamed of. Unluckily my commission was to write on the "Distress", so I couldn't do

J.M. Synge in Connemara, a drawing by Jack B. Yeats

anything like what I would have wished to do as an interpretation of the whole life. . . . There are sides of all that western life the groggy-patriot-publican-general shop man who is married to the priest's half-sister and is second cousin once-removed of the dispendary doctor, that are horrible and awful. This is the type that is running the present United Irish League anti-grazier campaign while they're swindling the people themselves in a dozen ways and then buying out their holdings and packing off whole families to America. . . . All that side of the matter of course I left untouched in my stuff. I sometimes wish to God I hadn't a soul and then I could give myself up to putting those lads on the stage. God, wouldn't they hop! In a way it is all heartrending, in one place the people are starving but wonderfully attractive and charming, and in another place where things are going well one has a rampant double-chinned vulgarity I haven't seen the like of.'

C. P. Scott wrote to Synge: 'You have done capitally for us, and with Mr Yeats have helped to bring home to people here the life of those remote districts as it can hardly have been done before.' Synge himself, however, remained dissatisfied and refused Whaley, a Dublin publisher, permission to reprint the articles in book form.

Two girls of Connemara. 'At every crossroads we passed groups of young healthy-looking boys and men amusing themselves with hurley or pitching, and further back on little heights, a small field's breadth from the road, there were many groups of girls sitting out by the hour, near enough to the road to see everything that was passing, yet far enough away to keep their shyness undisturbed. Their red dresses looked peculiarly beautiful among the fresh green of the grass and opening bracken, with a strip of sea behind them, and, far away, the grey cliffs of Clare.'
From Galway to Gorumna

The Blasket Islands, seen from Dunquin

It may have been because he felt it necessary to sink himself more completely into the life of the peasantry without specific motives that he went down to Kerry again in August, staying first with the Long family at Ballyferriter and then visiting the Great Blasket island, where he stayed with Padraig O'Cathain, the 'King' of the island. The last two weeks he again spent with Philly Harris at Mountain Stage, though in this cottage his asthma always troubled him. On his way back to Dublin he stopped at Coole, where his advice was needed about the reorganization of the Irish National Theatre Society in such a way that the choice of plays would no longer be made by the democratic vote of all the members. Fred Ryan and AE and Synge drew up new rules which should give three directors the power they needed, and the Irish National Theatre Society Limited came into being, with Yeats, Lady Gregory and Synge as directors. One of their first decisions was not to produce *The Tinker's Wedding*, as they felt it would be, in Yeats' words, 'dangerous at present'.

96

AFTER a long day's wandering I reached, towards the twilight, a little cottage on the south side of Dingle Bay, where I have often lived. There is no village near it; yet many other cottages are scattered on the little hills not far off; and as the people I lodge with are, in some ways, a leading family, many men and women look in during the day, or in the evening, to talk or tell stories, or to buy a few pennyworth of sugar or starch. Although this cottage is not on the road anywhere—the main road passes a few hundred yards to the west—it is well known also to the peculiar race of local respectable tramps who move from one family to another in some special neighbourhood or barony. This evening when I came in I found a little old man, in a tall hat, and long brown coat, sitting up on the settle beside the fire, who was spending, one could see, a night or more in the place.

I had a great deal to tell the people at first of my travels in different parts of the county, to the Blasket Islands—which they can see from here—Corkaguiney, and Tralee; and they had news to tell me also of people who have married or died since I was here before, or gone away, or come back from America. Then I was told that the old man, Dermot, or Darby, as he is called in English, was the finest story-teller in Iveragh; and after a while he told us a long story in Irish, but spoke so rapidly and indistinctly—he had no teeth—that I could understand but few passages, and most of the younger people, fairly good native Irish speakers, had difficulty also. When he finished, I asked him where he had heard the story.

"I heard it in the city of Portsmouth," he said. I worked there for fifteen years, and four years in Plymouth, and a long while in the hills of Wales; twenty-five years in all I was working at the other side; and there were many Irish in it, who would be telling stories in the evening, the same as we are doing here. I heard many good stories, but what can I do with them now, and I an old lisping fellow, the way I can't give them out like a ballad?"

When he had talked a little more about his travels, and a bridge over the Severn, that he thought the greatest wonder of the world, I asked him if he remembered the famine.

"I do well," he said. "I was living near Kenmare, and many's the day I saw them burying the corpses in the ditch by the road. It was after that I went to England; for this country was ruined and destroyed. I heard there was work at that time in Plymouth; so I went to Dublin, and took a boat that was going to England; but it was at a place called Liverpool they put me on shore, and then I had to walk to Plymouth, asking my way on the road. In that place I saw the soldiers after coming back from the Crimea, and they all broken and maimed." Then he turned to one of the men: "Do you know the story of the man who fished up the box of smoke. Theda?"

Corrected proof of the essay 'In West Kerry'

Sara Allgood, who created the parts of
Cathleen in *Riders to the Sea*, Molly
Byrne in *Well of the Saints*, Widow Quin
in the *Playboy* and the nurse Lavarcham
in *Deirdre*

The new arrangement caused some resentment among the actors, and a number
felt that the theatre was being led away from its original devotion to the Nationalist
movement. After a successful tour of Oxford, Cambridge and London they
returned to Dublin, and all but Sara and Molly Allgood, Arthur Sinclair and the
brothers Fay left the company. Some attempts at conciliation were made, but the
directors held out for the importance of artistic quality over political expediency
and the Fays were obliged to begin building up another company. This gave
Molly Allgood her opportunity, and in January 1906 she played Cathleen in
Riders to the Sea and was, according to Willie Fay, 'not at all bad'.

Synge was now very much involved in Abbey Theatre matters, reading proposed plays, attending rehearsals and coping with the multitude of small crises
that the theatre invariably produces. *Riders to the Sea* was revived on 30 January
1906. Maunsel & Company of Dublin were now publishing *The Aran Islands*
with illustrations by Jack Yeats, and J. M. Hone was thinking of publishing a
book of Synge's Kerry and Wicklow essays, first issuing some in his own magazine,
The Shanachie. Synge contributed an essay to each of issues 2–6 of this quarterly.
The proposed collection of essays, however, did not appear until after his death.

Molly Allgood (Maire O'Neill), who created the parts of Pegeen Mike in the *Playboy* and Deirdre in *Deirdre of the Sorrows*, which she also directed

*Synge and
Molly Allgood*

On 6 February Synge took rooms at 57 Rathgar Road, Rathgar, ostensibly to be nearer the theatre, but certainly also to give him the privacy he now needed for his relationship with Molly Allgood. Although now nearing his thirty-fifth birthday he was still fearful of his family's reaction to such an unsuitable friendship. Molly was not only a papist, but also an actress, and the Synge family regarded the theatre as sinful. None of his close relations ever attended plays, and only once, on 15 October 1906, when assured that no actual drama was to be performed, was young Edward Stephens allowed to go to the Abbey Theatre for a conversazione. Moreover, Molly was working class in origin and comparatively uneducated. There were too many counts against her. In February 1906, the company visited Wexford for a one-night stand, and it was then that Synge's feelings became obvious to his colleagues. He accompanied the actors also on their other one-night stands in Dundalk in March and May and on their week-long English tour in April, and the longer tour of Glasgow, Aberdeen, Newcastle-on-Tyne, Edinburgh (where he sat for a portrait by Joseph Paterson) and Hull in July. Intensely aware of the fifteen years' difference in their ages, he was jealous of Molly's enjoyment of the company of other men, and Udolphus ('Dossie') Wright, who was also attracted to her, was a particular source of discomfort.

Rathgar Road, Dublin, where Synge occupied rooms from February to May 1906

J. M. Synge in July 1906, a photograph taken during the Abbey Theatre Company's visit to Edinburgh

Lady Gregory hoped that Dossie would take Molly away from him and she and Yeats were both troubled by the situation. It was for them not only a matter of disparity of age, class and upbringing, but also a matter of a director falling in love with one of his own employees. Mercifully, however, Molly proved to be excellent as Nora in *In the Shadow of the Glen*, and an obvious candidate for Abbey stardom.

Their relationship was uneasy. Synge called her 'Changeling' because of her unpredictable changes of mood. She often upset him by going off for picnics with others, and by failing to write to him when she was away. She, for her part, found his jealousy maddening and his frequent descriptions of his distress at her thoughtlessness 'idiotic'. When together, walking the glens of Wicklow, they were often ecstatically happy, but quarrelled almost as often, for Molly had a quick temper and seems, at least on occasion, to have rather enjoyed making her lover buckle under.

The 'Playboy' begun Synge was now working on *The Playboy of the Western World*, which he had first made notes for in 1904. By the autumn he had the whole play mapped out and a good deal of dialogue written. He now saw it as a vehicle for Molly, and while Pegeen Mike's language owes a great deal to his Kerry friends, her temperament is not unlike that of his beloved. The waywardness, the wildness, the warmth, the independence, the sudden bursts of temper and the restless yet ill-informed ambition were all characteristic of Molly.

Synge went to Coole on 10 July 1906 to discuss with Yeats and Lady Gregory how to reinvigorate the theatre. A business secretary, W. A. Henderson, was hired, and at Yeats' insistence an English actress, a Miss Darragh, joined the

Waterford, Reginald's Tower

Bray, the Promenade

company, largely in order to act in Yeats' own plays, for which he felt the existing Irish actresses to be inadequate. Meanwhile, in the spring of 1906, Mrs Synge moved from Crosthwaite Park to Glendalough House in Glenageary to remain near to the Stephens family who had transferred themselves to Silchester Road. Here Synge was given a room of his own, and he gave up his Rathgar flat in May and returned home to work on the *Playboy*. He wrote to Molly almost every evening of the week, and at weekends or when she was not rehearsing they would travel to Bray by train and then walk out into the hills to find a place where they could lie in the bracken and make love. His letters are filled with longing for their next meeting, complaints of the inadequacy of her letters and fret over the impossibility of ever reconciling his family to their love. He tried to persuade her to educate herself by reading, as 'it will make life richer for both of us'. His mother being away, he ate at the Stephens' table, and reported gloomily, 'I don't fit well into that family party somehow – they are so rich and I am poor, and they are religious and I'm as you know, and so on with everything. . . . I don't like hanging about their house as a poor relation, although I'm a paying guest, as I know that they, or most of them, in their hearts despise a man of letters.'

Move to Glendalough House

On 25 August he set off once again for Kerry and Philly Harris' cottage, where he wrote constantly to Molly, did very little work, and returned to Dublin after eighteen days largely because he had had no word from her after one of his letters of complaint. Agnes Tobin, an American poet and patroness of the arts, was now in Dublin, and she and Synge went down to Waterford where her ancestors had

Agnes Tobin

come from. Molly was not pleased and that Sunday they quarrelled bitterly, but *Petrarch* were soon reconciled again. Miss Tobin had translated Petrarch's sonnets, and was constantly urging Synge to write poetry. At this time he did experiment in trans-lating some of Petrarch's *Sonnets to Laura in Death* into a cadenced prose which served later as the model for the language of *Deirdre of the Sorrows*. He seems to have told Miss Tobin about Molly at this time also. He wrote to Samuel of his intended marriage too, and was astonished at Samuel's expressing nothing but pleasure. He suffered more, indeed, from the vagaries of his mistress than the disapproval of his family. Quarrels and reconciliations followed each other that autumn, he insistent upon trying to educate her and even thinking of her as a potential playwright, she resentful of his schoolmasterly references to her inexperi-ence and irritated by his being unimpressed by her growing stature as an actress.

Engraving by J. M. Synge's cousin, Edward Synge

The Abbey Theatre Company in the 1906 production of Lady Gregory's *Hyacinth Halvey*. From left to right the players are: W. G. Fay, Arthur Sinclair, Frank Fay, J. A. O'Rourke, Brigit O'Dempsey and Sara Allgood

When he grew depressed over the last stages of the writing of the *Playboy*, however, she encouraged him, and she did in fact read some of the books he lent her. It was for Synge a stimulating if not always a happy relationship. He had learned to mock his own weaknesses to some extent, signing himself in his letters to her 'your old Tramp', and he began to recognize that her wildness was a part of her attraction. 'We're all wild geese, at bottom, all we players, artists and writers,' he told her, 'and there is no keeping us in a backyard like barndoor fowl.'

To the stresses attendant upon his love affair that autumn and winter were added those of illness and the struggle to complete the *Playboy*. He took the first two acts to Lady Gregory and Yeats on 13 November, but had too sore a throat to read them aloud himself. At last he invited Molly to his home to meet his mother, but she came the day after the one she was expected and Mrs Synge contrived to pretend that she was only one of his theatrical friends. His doctor advised him to take a rest, and he himself, with fever and slight congestion of the lung, again suspected tuberculosis. He spent fourteen days with his cousin Edward

Synge, an etcher, at Byfleet in Surrey and there he corrected the proofs of *The Aran Islands* and at last wrote to his mother about Molly. Mrs Synge did not reply immediately but wrote in her diary, 'I got a long letter from Johnnie telling me.' She had known all along. Molly, on her side, was nervous of Lady Gregory being told the situation. Mrs Synge, probably with more tact than truth, at last wrote to her son saying that she had thought the friend he had so often gone walking with had been male, but, after seeing how many letters he got, and seeing Molly's photograph she had suspected something. 'Then she says', Synge reported to Molly, 'it would be a good thing if it made me happier, and to wind up she points out how poor we shall be with our £100 a year. Quite a nice letter for a first go off.'

Although he had read the third act of the *Playboy* to Lady Gregory and Yeats on 28 November, he was still dissatisfied, and continued to work on it while in England.

Abbey Theatre
troubles

Meanwhile Miss Horniman, following the departure of Miss Darragh, and recognizing that Yeats' plays demanded different styles of acting and production from those of Synge and the other writers of peasant plays, hired Ben Iden Payne as director of the company. There were immediate ructions, and Synge, on his return to Dublin, had to be peace-maker. On 11 January, after many discussions, he drew up a proposal that Payne should be overall director and director of Yeats' plays, that Willie Fay should have an increase in salary and complete control of 'dialect work', and that the authors should have the right to withdraw their plays at the end of six months if the new arrangements proved unsatisfactory. To this all parties agreed, though Lady Gregory only accepted the new man for Yeats' sake, telling Synge that after all Yeats' work was 'more important than any other'. Yeats commented to her in a letter, 'I don't suppose Synge sympathised with your telling him that you cared most for my work. I really don't think him selfish or egotistical, but he is so absorbed in his own vision of the world that he cares for nothing else. But there is a passage in Nietzsche which describes this kind of man as if he were the normal man of genius. A woman here the other day told me that she said to Synge, "so and so thinks you the best of the Irish dramatists", to which he replied with a perfectly natural voice as if he were saying something as a matter of course, "That isn't saying much."' Miss Horniman was less understanding. She wrote to Lady Gregory: 'Mr Synge's letter made me really angry. It carried this to my mind – let us have a theatre where foreign classics and other plays may be used to train actors to play Synge. Let other authors go hang! The lessee has no vote, she is bound by her Saxon sense of honour, it is absurd that her views or desires should be regarded except when she admires and pushes Synge's plays.'

Jimmy. all's locked here, but ask them whether Guin is coming beyond. She'll have Draughts of her thinking madar in her now.

TJ. III / 818

4

-(Widow Quin comes in hastily,with a jar of poteen under her

shawl:she stands for a moment in astonishment when she sees Mahon -

Widow Quin-(to Mahon)-

(On has in A?)

You didn't go far at all?

Mahon

I seen the coasting steamer passing,and I got t cramp in my leg,so

I said the devil go along with him and turned again.

Widow Quin

And where is it you're travelling now?

Mahon

I'm not ~~thinking at all~~ *minding*, and it so droughty this day in the gleaming

sun.-(looking under her shawl)-(If it's the stuff you have)

give me a supeen for the love of God, and I destroyed tramping

since Tuesday was a week.

Widow Quin *(treating him ostentatiously as a sick child.)*

(a private end.) Sit down ~~then~~ *now* by the fire and take your ease for a space.-(giving

(would have a right to be destroyed indeed,)

him poteen)-May that be to your happiness and leaghth of life.

mahon

God increase you. -(drinks looking anto fire)--

Widow Quin-(going to men R.)-- *(quickly & stealthily to men)*

Do you know what? That man's a raving maniac would scare the world.

Jimmy-(with druenken wisdom)-

I was well night thinking that.

Page from a draft of *The Playboy of the Western World*

CAIRLEAN NA SEILMIDE

Slade
Dartmouth
Town England

Jan 11^(th)
190_

Dear Synge
   your letter Just come & hasten to
do you some Jockeys costumes

White
handkerchief
round neck

This was
the costume
That
"76 brave
Muldoons
used to wear

Home made
Jockey cap. with a long peak

(football Jersey

Tweed Trousers   (always tweed
stuffed in boots   or frieze Trousers
                    never white Jockey
                         breeches)

half wellington boots
not long boots. which are very
seldom seen except at the bigger
meetings

108

It was in this atmosphere of crisis and controversy that *The Playboy of the Western World* went into rehearsal on 8 January 1907. Lady Gregory, Yeats and Willie Fay were all nervous about it. Fay wanted the burning of Christy's leg to be omitted. Lady Gregory felt there were 'too many violent oaths'. Many cuts were made during the rehearsals which Synge supervised, but Willie Fay later reported, 'We might as well have tried to move the Hill of Howth as move Synge. That was his play, he said, and barring one or two jots and tittles of "bad language" that he grudgingly consented to excise, it was the play that with a great screwing up of courage we produced.' The jots and tittles, in fact, amounted to some fifty fragments including the reference to the Widow Quin having reared a black ram at her breast and that to the drunkenness at Michael Cassidy's wake. Synge himself, aware of the accusations he was likely to face, wrote a programme note claiming that he had used few words he had not heard among the country people in his Wicklow childhood and from the fishermen of Kerry and Mayo, and that the plot was suggested by 'an actual occurrence in the west'. It was not the wisest defence, for it sounded like a challenge and as a challenge it was accepted. As he sat in the stalls watching rehearsals, leaning forward, arms folded, his soft black hat pushed back on his head, two days before the opening, John Butler Yeats made a drawing of him. He had a bad cough and was exhausted.

◀ Letter from Jack B. Yeats with suggestions for the jockey costume Christy Mahon should wear in the third act of *The Playboy of the Western World*

Synge at a rehearsal of *The Playboy of the Western World* in January 1907, drawn by John Butler Yeats

The Playboy of the Western World opened on 26 January 1907 with Maire O'Neill (Molly Allgood) as Pegeen Mike, Willie Fay as Christy Mahon and Sara Allgood as the Widow Quin. The first two acts were played without trouble, but during the third act the audience grew restless, and when Willie Fay, whose poor memory for his lines Synge had noted earlier, substituted 'Mayo girls' for 'chosen females' in the line, 'drifts of chosen females standing in their shifts', there was uproar. Once again Synge had cast a slur on Irish womanhood. Joseph Holloway, a steady supporter of the company, recorded in his journal that he thought Synge 'the evil genius of the Abbey'. The *Irish Times* thought the dialogue contained 'indiscretions', but the *Freeman's Journal* returned to the old complaint and called the play an 'unmitigated, protracted libel upon Irish peasant men and, worse still upon Irish girlhood'. It referred to the production as 'squalid' and to the language as 'barbarous jargon' and to the characters as 'repulsive creatures'. For the next performance Lady Gregory called in the police, but the audience was so noisy and abusive that the actors merely mouthed many of the lines, and defiantly bowed to their hostile audience at the end of each act. Once the curtain was rung down for the police to deal with the apparent ringleaders of the riot. At another point,

The End of the Race, a print by Jack B. Yeats commonly regarded as illustrating *The Playboy of the Western World*

Willie Fay stopped the play altogether and told the audience to get their money back and go away. No one present heard more than a few stray words of the whole production. Interviewed afterwards, Synge, excited and distrait, talking with great rapidity, tried to explain his intentions to a reporter, and when asked what he intended to do about the play in view of the night's experience, was reported as saying, 'We shall go on with the play to the very end in spite of all. I don't care a rap!' It was not a tactful remark to make. The following day W. B. Yeats returned to Dublin, arranged for more police and organized a claque of students to counter opposition to the play. He told the *Freeman's Journal* that the opposition came from people who 'had no books in their houses' and whose opinions had been formed by 'commonplace and ignorant people'. The play would not only last out the week but be staged for a further week after which he, Yeats, would 'lecture on the freedom of the theatre and invite our opponents to speak on its slavery to the mob if they've a mind to'. Synge said that the play had been suggested by an incident in Aran and also by the case of a man called Lynchehaun who had been hidden from the police in Achill.

Tuesday's performance was more riotous than ever. Some of Yeats' Trinity

111

"THE PLAYBOY."

LAST NIGHT'S PERFORMANCE

Leads to Further Disorderly Scenes

THE POLICE PRESENT IN FORCE

With the one exception that more of the comedy was heard by a certain section of the audience there was little change in the attitude of the protesting element last evening at the Abbey Theatre, when, for the fourth time, Mr. J. M. Synge's work, "The Playboy of the Western world," was produced. It may have been that the dissenting ones were not so strong, but they were very powerful in voice and action, and forming in a body on the right-hand side of the pit, they made things very unpleasant at intervals, and succeeded in creating a rather lively scene at the fall of the final curtain. On the other hand, there was an immense muster of the critical and intelligent public in the stalls and balcony, and the influence of these and the presence of about 50 police in the house had no doubt a deterrent effect on the sustained vocal and tramping efforts of the objectors.

ANOTHER PROTEST.

Long before 8 o'clock the theatre was packed. The first unpleasant note came before the rise of the curtain on "Riders to the Sea," when an aged gentleman stood up in the balcony and commenced to deliver an address. He said he had come to utter a protest against Mr. Synge's "Playboy" and to demonstrate his respect for the virtue of the West of Ireland. He further stated that he intended to leave the house before the objectionable piece opened.

He was not allowed to carry out his intention, as he suggested, and in a couple of minutes he was outside the theatre on the far side of the street, with a couple of dozen policemen around him. The police were hissed for removing him. "Riders to the Sea" was again re-ceived with wrapt attention, and at its close all the artistes were heartily applauded as they came before the curtain.

After a fifteen minutes' interval Mr. W. B. Yeats and Mr. Synge came into the stalls, and the boys at the back rose up in a mass and hissed them. Then when the curtain went up there was an attempt to renew the disorder, but a stentorian voice overhead called for a fair hearing for the work, and, to the tune of "By the Banks of the Zuyder Zee," whistled by the young men at the rere, the comedy was commenced.

For some time things went harmoniously, the only noise being hisses and boohs for Messrs. Yeats and Synge as they left the auditorium for the stage. Mr. Synge re-turned again in a few minutes, and re-ceived a very mixed reception.

RENEWED UPROAR.

There was peace again until the entrance of "Christopher Mahon." Hoarse shouts were raised as he appeared at the doorway, and during his time on the stage it was not possible to hear a fourth of his lines. "Get off, you fraud," and "What do yo know of the West of Ireland?" were th cries that punctuated the hissing, groaning, and tramping; and great cheers were raised when Christie retired. When he reappeared he was met with cries of "Lynchehaun" and "Rotten," and amidst a perfect storm of hisses and clatter of feet the curtain fell. All this time Mr. Yeats was continuously running up and down a few flights of steps near the stage door, making exits and entrances without number, and these peripatetic movements became so marked that during the interval there were vigorous requests for "a cake walk by Mr. W. B. Yeats," but that gentleman appeared only to take a quiet seat in the stalls.

When the comedy was resumed the house appeared more inclined to disorder, and in one or two instances it was noticed that the dialogue was expunged at some of the objectionable parts. At each of these places the cry at once came—"Who cut the comedy?" and when Mr. Synge was again seen in the stalls he was told to take his "miserable effort to England at once."

But the first great outburst of disorder came when "Christopher Mahon" pro-ceeded to tell the story of the murder of his father. "Lynchehaun" came freely to many tongues in the house, and as the narrative proceeded it was punctuated with interjections of "Hit him," "Brain him," and "Get him arrested by the bobbies who are behind the scenes." Various melodies were subsequently whistled by the occu-pants of the pit, and, strange to say, the curtain fell amidst all-round applause.

A STORM OF HISSES.

During the next interval there were many discussions in the house, and as the police were drafted into all parts in num-bers the boys in the back heartily whistl "The Peeler and the Goat."

A small scuffle took place at the back the pit between two enthusiasts, and member of a party in the stalls invited other to the street to "fight it out." latter responded and the would-pugilists, attended by many admirers, o got to the vestibule before the police interfered.

Just before the curtain went up for final act Mr. Yeats and a few policem came into the stalls amidst a storm hisses, and as a sergeant threatened to move a certain member of the audience was treated to a number of uncompliment-ary remarks.

Early in the scene one of the members of the company tells a story about wh skulls and yellow skulls and black sku in the Dublin Museum, and as Mr. Syn returned to the stalls just at this poin voice from the pit roared—"Twon't without his numbskull," a rema which caused immense laughter among young men behind.

In the scene where the old man, suppo to be murdered, appears looking for son, who is concealed behind the door, asks in a rich brogue if the lady of house saw "a strap of a boy, black, very dirty, anywhere?" Whatever reply in the book is no one heard it tight, for a voice upstairs promptly returned—"He is behind the door, old cha

ROARS OF LAUGHTER.

There were roars of laughter all over house at this sally, but things changed, there was great disorder, while the po arrested one of the audience, and remo um for creating a disturbance.

The last curtain fell amidst a perf pandemo ium. Young men lit cigaret counted the seats, and blocked up all exits, while others lucidly called for speec from Messrs. Yeats and Synge. These g tlemen appeared but neither spoke, the police promptly set about clearing house, a proceeding which was atten with great noise, punctuated here and with the sounds of a bugle in the galle protest or two was made from the ba and just as the occupants of the stalls w nearly out, Mr. Monahan called over seats and asked for a hearing. The lat sented, and was told that all Irishm he loved their country protested again the further production of "The Playb e Western World."

Mr. Yeats, in reply, said—"It is too now for speeches or protests, but come here on Monday week and say all you on the subject."

While the theatre was being cleared the police after the performance, crowds of people flocked from O'Con street and other neighbouring thoro fares, and surrounded the building. ing on the orders of Superintendent By a squad of police promptly charged crowd, and after some difficulty succee in turning them towards O'Connell str and eventually dispersing them. Fort ately none of the disorderly scenes of previous night were witnessed.

AN ORATION BEFORE THE
PERFORMANCE
AND
ITS
SEQUEL

A FOREIGN VISITOR
STOLIDY CONTEMPLATING
THE SCENE

OBJECTS TO THE
POLICE AND
FEELS PUT OUT

ON THE STAGE
AN ACCIDENTAL VIEW
OF A REAL INSPECTOR ON
DUTY OUTSIDE THE PUB DOOR

AFTER THE PLAY
THE ACTORS BECOME THE
AUDIENCE.

ARGUMENTS FOR AND
AGAINST
FOLLOWED
BY

AN INVITATION
OUTSIDE

FUTURE OF THE PLAY

Lady Gregory, seen last evening, said that the directors of the Theatre intended to continue to produce "The Playboy" until it was given a fair hearing. There was hope, she said, in the attention accorded it last night, and if matters improved it would come off on Saturday night as originally intended. Otherwise it would be repeated as long as necessary.

Messrs. Yeats and Synge declared that they have nothing to add to the remarks already published from them.

Mr. W. G. Fay agreed with Lady Gregory, and said that although he had no personal interest in the play beyond that of an artist, he believed it should be continued until it was made or killed by a responsible audience and not by a crowd of young men who paid their money to amuse themselves and prevent the play getting a fair hearing.

The *Evening Herald* report of events at the fourth performance of *The Playboy of the Western World*, 31 January 1907

College claque were drunk, and one of them was thrown out by Synge and others after a fist fight had developed. This struck Holloway as amusingly ironic. Hugh Lane pointed out offenders to the police who were led in by Yeats and several people were arrested. The Trinity claque ended the evening by climbing on stage and singing 'God Save the King', while others sang 'A Nation Once Again'. Yeats shouted at the audience, 'We have put this play before you to be heard and to be judged. Every man has a right to hear it and condemn it if he pleases, but no man has a right to interfere with another man hearing a play and judging for himself. The country that condescends either to bully or to permit itself to be bullied soon ceases to have any fine qualities. . . .'

Wednesday and Thursday night brought an increase in the number of police and in the audibility of the performance, and Friday night and Saturday night were fairly quiet, but only, it seems, because the patrons had no wish to appear in court the next day. Griffith, now editor of *Sinn Fein*, a weekly paper, had been obliged to hold off until Saturday. When he did have his opportunity he took it, accusing the play of foul language and supporting his allegation by misquotation.

The Poet addressed the Audience.

"I Don't Care a Rap."

Caricatures of W. B. Yeats and J. M. Synge published
in *The Abbey Row*

PROGRAMME.

THE ABBEY ROW.

NOT Edited by W. B. YEATS.

The customary cover of the Abbey Theatre programme, and (right) the cover of *The Abbey Row*

Several entertained Dubliners produced a pamphlet, *The Abbey Row*, whose cover was a caricature of the cover of the Abbey Theatre's occasional magazine, *The Arrow*, and which contained much good-humoured mockery of all the proceedings. William Boyle withdrew his plays from the Abbey. Letters of attack continued to be published. Synge, exhausted, retired to bed. He did not attend the public discussion of the play on Monday night when Yeats again showed his courage and loyalty in the face of an angry and vociferous audience.

Throughout the following weeks resolutions condemning the *Playboy* were passed by Irish groups in Liverpool and by other groups in Ireland itself. Arthur Griffith and Padraic Pearse both announced that the 'Anglo-Irish Theatre' was now dead and that a truly Irish theatre was now needed. In this comment one can see some of the cause of the disturbance. The Nationalists may have felt that a play which described an Irish girl making a hero of a man who had killed his father was not anything but a hindrance in their movement to make Ireland proud of its nationhood and eager for freedom from the English yoke. They were also suspicious, however, of both Yeats and Synge as members of the Anglo-Irish Protestant ascendancy, and suspected that Synge's interest in the Irish peasantry was that felt by a superior being in the picturesque oddity of his inferiors. They

The Abbey Row

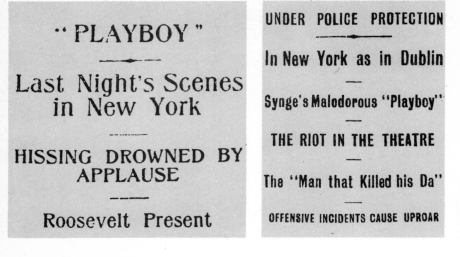

The Playboy in New York, headlines from the *Evening Telegraph* and *Evening Herald* 29 November 1911

found caricature where he had intended glorification and suspected reportage where he had intended fable. Synge, now ill in bed with influenza, made no more public statements. During the height of the row he had written to the *Irish Times* to correct the impression given by the report of his first-night interview. He had said: '*The Playboy of the Western World* is not a play with "a purpose" in the modern sense of the word, but although parts of it are, or are meant to be, extravagant comedy, still a great deal more that is behind it, is perfectly serious when looked at in certain light. That is often the case, I think, with comedy and no one is quite sure whether "Shylock" and "Alceste" should be played seriously or not. There are, it may be hinted, several sides to *The Playboy*.'

It was not for some years that his comment was to be taken seriously. Riots attended the play in America after his death, and even as late as 1950 a writer in *Envoy* dismissed his work by saying: 'Irish resentment of his work is instinctive and well-grounded in the mysticism of the Gael. . . . He observed superficial traits, the heroes, clowns and playboys, on the Irish scene, but unfortunately he had little inkling of how they lived or thought between the acts. . . . The freakish nature of the taste that has tended to be sympathetic towards [him] was cultivated by Yeats. It is Ascendancy or pseudo-Ascendancy, taste. One had to be above to appreciate in full the antics of the natives. His work is unlikely to have any bearing, except in a negative way, on the future of literature in this country.'

Synge was not now to be tempted into further comments. After recovering from his illness he worked on his essays for *The Shanachie* and helped nurse his mother who had caught the infection. He was now seriously thinking about *Deirdre of the Sorrows*. He had written to Molly from England in December: 'My next play must be quite different from the P. Boy. I want to do something quiet and stately and restrained and I want you to act in it.' He had a little earlier sent her *Cuchulain of Muirthemne* and advised her to read the story of the Sons of Usnach. He was not yet ready, or indeed well enough, to begin, however. On 1 March he fell ill again. On 9 March he told Molly: 'My mother was talking the other day about our marriage and how we intended to get on. She is still rather frightened at our poverty, but she is much more rational about it than she was. You must have charmed her!' Charles Frohman was due to come to Dublin to select plays for American production, and Synge was angered to hear that only *Riders to the Sea* of all his plays was to be shown to him. He wrote to Frank Fay to ask how many times *Spreading the News*, *In the Shadow of the Glen*, *Riders to the Sea* and *On Baile's Strand* had been played by the Abbey, and told Molly, 'I expect their pieces have been done at least three times as often as mine. If that is so there'll be a row.' Fay replied sensibly and practically and there was no row. On 24 March he was well enough to walk with Molly, but soon collapsed again. He wrote an intemperate *Letter to the Gaelic League* for its short-sighted campaign for the speaking of Irish, but Yeats persuaded him not to publish it. His neck glands had begun to swell again and he felt obliged to postpone his marriage plans. He wrote to Stephen MacKenna on 9 April that he had been 'ill for two months – four weeks not even downstairs', and added, 'I sometimes wish I had never left my garret in the rue d'Assas – it seems funny to write the words again – the scurrility, and ignorance and treachery of some of the attacks upon me have rather disgusted me with the middle class Irish Catholic. As you know I have the wildest admiration for the Irish Peasants, and for Irish men of known or unknown genius – do you bow? – but between the two there's an ungodly ruck of fat faced, sweaty headed swine. They are in Dublin and in Kingstown, and also in all the country towns. Do you know that the B[oards] of Guardians all over the west and south have been passing resolutions condemning me and the French Government? Irish humour is dead, MacKenna, and I've got influenza.'

Illness

On 25 April he got the advanced copies of *The Aran Islands* at last published by Maunsel. He sent Masefield a copy and in his letter of thanks Masefield said, 'I meant to write you at the time of your trouble at the theatre, as I feared that the bitterness of the fools who attacked you might have discouraged you; but Yeats made the uproar so much of a comedy that I did not send the letter. There are a lot of damned fools in the world. As a rule we can ignore them. But when they try to impose their cock-old laws upon the artist they need a strong jolt. I am glad that they got it at the Abbey Theatre.'

'The Aran Islands' published

Synge did not accompany the Abbey Theatre on their May 1907 tour of England when they visited Glasgow, Cambridge, Birmingham, Oxford and London, deciding to join them for the London performance only. The Lord

Chamberlain's office proved to be nervous about the *Playboy* and asked for details of the Dublin riots, so, fearful the Irish of Birmingham might give him cause to withdraw his licence, Yeats decided to put it on only in Oxford and London. Synge was furious. He told Molly, who, like the other players, was curious about this decision: 'It was withdrawn for political reasons I believe, I am not satisfied with the way things are going in the company . . . and I wrote to Yeats yesterday proposing to resign my directorship. . . .' Yeats himself was angered at Synge's letter and said acidly, 'While we are fighting your battles is hardly the moment to talk of resignation.'

The 'Playboy' in Oxford and London

The Playboy of the Western World opened at Oxford on 5 June. Synge was staying with Jack Yeats in Devon, having arrived there on 30 May, and missed the first performance of his play before an appreciative audience. He was, however, present for the opening night of 8 June in the Great Queen Street Theatre, London. The play was an immediate and resounding success. Synge and the players were invited everywhere. He was invited to the House of Commons by Stephen Gwynn, had dinner with Masefield and supper with Lord Dunraven. Thanks to the courage and obstinacy of Yeats, and the equal courage and ability of the Abbey Theatre Company, the battle to establish Synge as a dramatist of genius had at last been won.

In Ireland that summer Synge did not go to Tomrilands House with his mother but took a month's holiday in the Wicklow Mountains at Mrs McGuirk's cottage in Glencree. He went there on 28 June and Molly and Sara stayed in another cottage half a mile away. Quarrels seemed to have been forgotten. Synge was writing poetry again and also reworking older poems. The girls returned to Dublin on 11 July, but Molly came back for another fortnight on 23 July. They were both very happy, and only the thought of the forthcoming operation on Synge's neck, which had been scheduled for September, prevented them planning a definite date for marriage. On 4 August they returned to Dublin, and on 11 August the company set out on a tour of Waterford, Cork and Kilkenny, though of Synge's plays only *Riders to the Sea* was to be presented. Synge was distressed at this. 'One thing is certain,' he wrote Molly, 'I'm not going to kill myself anymore for the Theatre. I get no thanks for it, on any side, and I do no good – at least as things are going now.' He grew suspicious and jealous of Molly again and could do no work. He developed another bad cough and had to cancel a planned trip to Brittany. On 12 September his doctor examined him and the next day he wrote to Molly: 'I feel perfectly hard, and fearless and defiant now . . .

Another operation

I'm going in there to be cured, I hope.' On 14 September he went into hospital. The operation was successful, but it could not cure him. He had eighteen months more to live.

118

On a Birth-day.

Lark of Ronsard, Geoffrey Chauces,
Nashe and Patch, the poaching courser,
Lark of Heywood, Creen, and Beaumont,
Lark of Kerry, Meath, and Thomond,
Heard from Smyrna and Sahara
To the surf of Connemara,
Lark of April, June and May
Sing loudly this my Lady-day.

Friend of Ronsard, Nashe and Beaumont
Lark of Ulster, Meath and Thomond
Heard from Smyrna and Sahara
To the surf of Connemara
Lark of april, June, and May
Sing loudly this my Lady Day

Draft of 'On a Birth-day', written for Molly Allgood in 1908

Synge left the hospital on 25 September, 1907, happy at the success of the operation, and full of plans for his marriage and the writing of his play on the Sons of Usnach. A year later, he celebrated the day of his release in an anniversary poem whose message is grim but whose tone is almost cavalier. Though he knew now that he was losing the struggle against illness and death, he felt that at least he was putting up a good fight.

> I've thirty months, and that's my pride,
> Before my age's a double score,
> Though many lively men have died
> At twenty-nine or little more.
>
> I've left a long and famous set
> Behind some seven years or three,
> But there are millions I'd forget
> Will have their laugh at passing me.

The writing of 'Deirdre'

He dated it carefully 25 September. It was a day to remember. On 12 October he went to stay at Thady Kevane's cottage in Ventry, County Kerry, but at night his asthma gave him so much trouble that he was forced to return to Dublin four days later. There he worked steadily and rapidly and on 1 November had managed to reorganize *Deirdre* from four acts into three. On 24 November the Abbey company went on tour to Manchester, Glasgow and Edinburgh. Both Synge's one-act plays were performed in Manchester, but only *In the Shadow of the Glen* in Edinburgh. The company was restless and Willie Fay no longer had the authority to control it. Synge was no longer the stalwart supporter of Fay that he had been. He may have been influenced by Molly or by the company's continuing neglect of *The Well of the Saints* and the *Playboy*. He was, in any case, obsessed now with *Deirdre*, and on 1 December wrote to Molly that he had completed the seventh draft of the third act and that the play could now be read all through. The next day he met with Lady Gregory and Yeats, and the latter told him that the stars foretold a 'very big event in his life was due the next month', and added, 'If you were a different sort of man I'd say it was a wild imprudent love affair.' It may have been intended as a warning. On 4 December the three directors met together again and proposed that the company should elect a committee of three to 'consult with the Stage Manager and Directors as to the rules of Discipline', and that these rules should then be vetted by the whole company. This arrangement did not give Willie Fay the authority he needed, and after further discussions, threatened resignations and confusions, he resigned from the company on 13 January 1908.

Charles Ricketts' designs for the costumes of Molly Byrne and Timmy the Smith, for the 1908 production of *Well of the Saints*

Meanwhile, on 6 December 1907, Synge began to feel pains in his side. They increased in intensity over the next few days but the doctors could find nothing wrong. In January 1908 he found a flat at 47 York Road, Rathmines, for Molly and himself to live in after their marriage. He moved into it himself on 2 February. His internal pains had eased somewhat and in February and March he was much involved with Yeats in running the Abbey Theatre, and himself directed performances of Lady Gregory's translations of Sudermann's *Teja* (March) and Molière's *The Rogueries of Scapin* (April). *The Tinker's Wedding* was published by Maunsel at this time, and in sending a copy to Joseph Paterson he said, 'we think it too dangerous to put on in the Abbey'. Plans for the wedding were going ahead, though Annie Stephens was so opposed to it that Mrs Synge could not mention it to her, and Edward Synge thought it financially impracticable.

Wedding plans

On 28 April the doctors found a lump in Synge's side; he again entered the Elpis Nursing Home on 30 April, having postponed his wedding plans, and was to be operated on on 4 May. On 3 May he wrote to Molly, 'My dearest love – this is a mere line for you my poor child, in case anything goes wrong with me tomorrow, to bid you goodbye and ask you to be brave and good, and not to forget the good times we've had and the beautiful things we've seen together. Your Old Friend.' The operation, however, did not take place, and the letter remained unposted. Exploratory surgery revealed that the tumour was inoperable. Sir Charles Ball, the surgeon, feared for Synge's life, but his will to live was strong, and though Molly, fearing the worst, removed his effects from his flat and took them to Glendalough House on 25 May, by 24 June his mother was able to report that he looked well and weighed 176 pounds. On 6 July he was discharged from hospital and went to stay with the Stephens, his mother having gone to Tomrilands House for the summer. Once again several of his nurses wrote to him. Slowly he began to take walks and to think more about *Deirdre*. He had a slight relapse on 2 August and when Yeats visited him on 5 August he was still too sick to be able to concentrate on theatre matters. On 12 August he wrote sadly to MacKenna, 'The doctors say I'm a very interesting case and generally patronise my belly – to think that I used once to write "Playboys", MacKenna and now I'm a bunch of interesting bowels.'

He moved back to Glendalough House on 13 August. 'My poor mother,' he wrote to Molly, 'is not at all well and is in bed still. This illness seems to have aged her in some way, and she seems quite a little old woman with an old woman's voice. It makes me sad. It is sad also to see all our little furniture stowed away in these rooms. It is a sad queer time for us all, dear Heart, I sometimes feel inclined to sit down and wail.' Nevertheless he again took up his *Deirdre* typescripts and decided on 24 August to turn the play from three acts into two. There was now a possibility of an American edition of his plays being published, and when George Roberts came to discuss this with him he read him some of his poems. Roberts suggested that Maunsel should publish them, so Synge sent them to Yeats for his opinion. On 8 September Yeats wrote: 'Can you come and see me on Wednesday afternoon at Nassau (say) three o'clock. Some of the poems are very fine. I want to talk about them.' Synge was overjoyed, for he had been very nervous of showing them to Yeats. He was also pleased that Yeats wanted to publish them in a limited edition from the Cuala Press. George Roberts who had, after all, thought up the project, was less pleased. Synge told him that if it was a question of Maunsel *or* the Cuala Press publishing the poems then he would stick with his original agreement with Maunsel, but Roberts gave in to Yeats, and agreed to publish a more comprehensive trade edition to follow the limited Cuala one. Synge signed

POEMS AND TRANSLATIONS
BY JOHN M. SYNGE

CUALA PRESS
CHURCHTOWN
DUNDRUM
MCMIX

Title-page of *Poems and Translations*, published in an edition of 250 copies on 8 April 1909

the contract for this on 5 October, having sent a typescript of the book to Yeats on 2 October.

The book was to include a prose translation of Villon, *Prayer of the Old Woman, Villon's Mother* which touchingly reflects Synge's anxiety for his mother's health and his newly aroused understanding of her indestructible faith. It ended:

> *It's yourself bore Jesus, that has no end or death,*
> *and He the Lord Almighty, that took our weakness*
> *and gave Himself to sorrow, a young and gentle man.*
> *It's Himself is our Lord surely, and it's in that*
> *faith I'll live always.*

Molly was now busy with performances of a new play and Synge, at home alone with his ill mother, felt a sudden need to visit Germany once more. He must have known his mother was dying, but was not strong enough to face that crisis. Just as in the past he had avoided confrontations by telling both Samuel and his mother of his marriage plans by letter rather than face to face, so now he could not

123

help evading the issue. Moreover he himself was weak and ill and his mind was turning nostalgically to the healthy days of his youth, as it had the previous year turned to thoughts of Paris after the exhaustion of the *Playboy* riots. He set out on 6 October, and in London was obliged to stay in 'a sort of boarding house', being unable to find room in a hotel. He spent much of the following day sitting in Hyde Park. He arrived at Coblenz on 8 October and found the von Eiken sisters as kind as ever, but growing old. 'My friend is nice still,' he told Molly, 'but you needn't be uneasy. I am beginning to count the days till I can get back to you.' He wrote her a poem, a free version of an old Irish lyric:

Last visit to Germany

> *Some go to game, or pray in Rome*
> *I travel for my turning home*
>
> *For when I've been six months abroad*
> *Faith your kiss would brighten God*

He walked in the woods thinking of Deirdre in Alban, and sat on the banks of the Rhine, and thought further about Deirdre. On 16 October he wrote Molly, 'I am very sad tonight as I have just got very sad news of my poor old mother. She is much worse I am afraid – if she does not soon get better I shall have no one in the world but you. . . . Her life is little happiness to her now, and yet one cannot bear the idea of not having her with us any more. If she gets worse I will go home, perhaps, very soon. I do not like to think of her all by herself in the house.'

The next news of his mother was better, however, and he remained in Germany, reading Walther von der Vogelweide and translating a poem of his into prose to send to Molly. On 26 October Mrs Synge died. He did not feel equal to returning to Ireland for the funeral. He did not in fact return until 7 November. The loss of his mother affected him profoundly. She had been throughout his life a fixed and unwavering point of reference. His intellectual rejection of her beliefs had been complete but he had never lost his emotional dependence upon her presence, and now he wrote to Molly: 'People like Yeats who sneer at old fashioned goodness and steadiness in women seem to want to rob the world of what is most sacred in it. I cannot tell you how unspeakably sacred her memory seems to me. There is nothing in the world better or nobler than a single-hearted wife and mother. I wish you had known her better.' He even added, 'It makes me rage when I think of the people who go on as if art and literature and writing were the first things in the world. There is nothing so great and sacred as what is most simple in life.'

Death of Mrs Synge

Nevertheless, he himself was now working as hard as he was able. On 25 November Elizabeth Yeats wrote that she wished to omit 'The Curse' and 'Danny' from his book. Once again his forthrightness and violence of speech had upset

J.M. Synge in Coblenz, 1908

the squeamish. He seems to have agreed without rancour. He was now trying to make *Deirdre of the Sorrows* more vigorous and dramatic by extending the character of Owen, and the speeches he was now writing over and over again show how his own personal experiences and sufferings were being fitted into the play. Asked by Deirdre what Conchubor is doing, Owen replies, 'Stretching his belly and losing his hair.' At another point Owen says, 'I've been three weeks waiting in the bogs below, getting ague and asthma.' Later still Owen is made to say '[When] a man's [blood] does get cool he's jealous of stars and moon, jealous of his ass and dog and jealous of the sun and wind.' And again he says, 'Though I play the fool I'm no fool Deirdre, saving I'd liefer be bleaching in a bog hole, than living onward without a touch [of] kindness from your eyes and voice. It's a cold thing missing your chances from Inishmaan to the plain of Meath and you so lonesome you're ready to squeeze kisses on a cur dog's nose.' Deirdre's lament over Naisi is Synge's lament for his own death, and also, perhaps, a speech he wished Molly herself to make over him. 'Draw a little back with the squabbling

125

of fools when I am broken up with misery,' she cries, and one is reminded of Molly telling Synge that September that she would not go to his funeral because she would not be able to bear to see him dead and others living. This he had made into a poem which Yeats thought 'magnificent'.

> I asked if I got sick and died, would you
> With my black funeral go walking too,
> If you'd stand close to hear them talk or pray
> While I'm let down in that steep bank of clay.
>
> And, No, you said, for if you saw a crew
> Of living idiots, pressing round that new
> Oak coffin – they alive, I dead beneath
> That board – you'd rave and rend them with your teeth.

On 24 November Synge had an almost complete version of the second act. On 29 November the company went to Belfast for a week, and he was unhappy at Molly visiting Dossie Wright's relations in Balbriggan on her way back. He complained more of his health than of her wilfulness now, however, but Molly, perhaps with instinctive wisdom, would not countenance self-pity; he agreed that she was right, though he added, 'I think I owe it to myself to let you know that if I am so "self-pitiful" I have some reason to be so, as Dr Parsons' report of my health, though uncertain, was much more unsatisfactory than I thought it well to tell you. I only tell you now because I am unable to bear the thought that you should think of me with the contempt I saw in your face yesterday.' He was now aware that he was dying, and at the end of November he wrote:

> I read about the Blaskets and Dunquin,
> The Wicklow towns and fair days I've been in.
> I read of Galway, Mayo, Aranmore,
> And men with kelp along a wintry shore.
> Then I remember that that 'I' was I,
> And I'd a filthy job – to waste and die.

On poetry He had now finished writing the preface to his poems in which he talked of Villon and Herrick and Burns using 'the whole of their personal life as their material', and argued that 'Even if we grant that exalted poetry can be kept successful by itself, the strong things of life are needed in poetry also, to show that what is exalted or tender, is not made by feeble blood. It may almost be said that before verse can be human again it must learn to be brutal.' He was describing his own use of personal experience in his work and his own attempt to strengthen the

St Patrick's Cathedral, Dublin, where Synge took Molly Allgood for the Christmas Eve service in 1908

elegiac and stately *Deirdre of the Sorrows* by the introduction of coarse and violent passages.

In January proofs of the poems arrived and Edward Stephens, who had no idea that Synge wrote poetry, discovered him correcting them. Edward wrote later, 'His poems seemed so intimate that I was surprised at his willingness to publish them, and was so much embarrassed by his showing them to me that I could form no detached view of what I read. I did not know what to say, but he did not seem to expect me to say anything.' Synge never expected his relations to understand his work. Of all of them, only his cousin Florence Ross ever went to the theatre.

He was now engaged in sorting out his papers for his heirs, destroying much, but leaving a great deal, some marked 'for Biographical information'. He went with Molly to the Christmas Eve service at St Patrick's Cathedral, but his pain grew worse and his strength was ebbing. On 31 January he went into Elpis Nursing Home again. There was no question of operating. On 13 February

Christmas 1908

127

Edward M. Stephens,
J. M. Synge's nephew and
later biographer

Maunsel's announcement of the publication ▶
of Synge's works in four volumes

Synge's grave in Mount Jerome cemetery,
Dublin. 'There'll come a season when you'll
stretch / Black boards to cover me: / Then in
Mount Jerome I will lie, poor wretch, / With
worms eternally.' *To the Oaks of Glencree*

Preparing Harry Stephens came and visited him and helped him make out his Will. He
for death left all his manuscripts, royalties and property to his nephews Edward Stephens
(Harry's son), and Hutchinson Synge. To Molly he bequeathed a lifetime annuity
of £80 which would be reduced to £52 if she married. It was not even the total
income from his share of the estate inherited from his mother, for, as he had told
Molly earlier, that amounted to £110 a year income from a £1,500 share of the
property; and he had said in November, 'The £1,500 is, I think, really mine
not for my life only, so I will have that to leave you.' It does not seem entirely
improbable that Harry Stephens may have represented to Synge the inadvisability
of diminishing the family holdings by a direct bequest of a portion of them. His
own and his wife's dislike of the alliance with Molly was considerable, and family
solidarity was a matter of some importance to him.

Molly herself, after visiting him daily, left with the company for a week in
Manchester on 14 February. Synge asked his sister, Annie Stephens, to write to
her, as he had not the strength. She wrote on 17 and 19 February and reported
finding him 'a little better'. She did not tell Molly that everyone knew him to be
near death. When Molly did return on 22 February she went to see him immediately and then, in despair and anguish, sought out priest after priest to have a mass

said for his recovery. The priests could not understand why she wished for a mass to be said for a Protestant and none was said. She visited him every day till the end.

On the night of 23 March Elizabeth Yeats, still struggling to bring out Synge's *Poems and Translations*, had a dream, and said to her brother at breakfast: 'I think it will be all right with Synge, for last night I saw a galley struggling with a storm and then it shot into calm and bright sunlight and I heard the keel grate on the shore.' The ship she saw was not a real ship, but 'like the "Shadowy waters" ship on the Abbey stage, a sort of allegorical thing. There was also a girl in a bright dress, but she seemed to vanish as the ship ran ashore; all about the girl, and indeed everything, was broken and confused until the bow touched the shore in bright sunlight.'

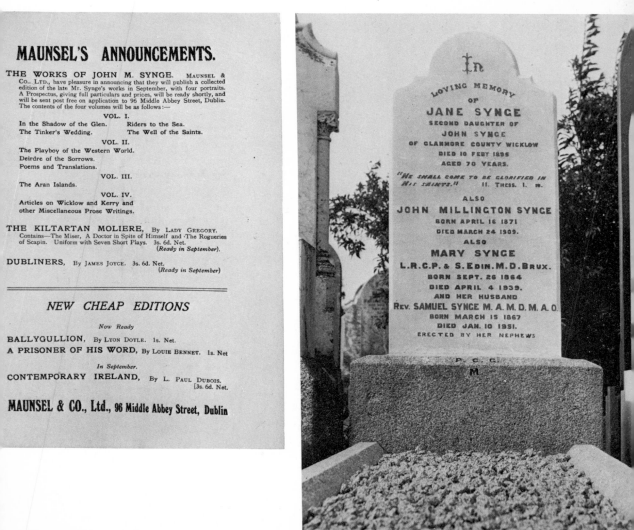

Synge died at 5.30 a.m. on 24 March 1909. Robert Synge refused Yeats' request to have a death mask made, and at the funeral the Synge family, in formal black, stood apart from the other group of Synge's colleagues and friends. The volume of *Poems and Translations* appeared on 8 April. *Deirdre of the Sorrows*, edited from the manuscripts by Lady Gregory, Yeats and Molly, was first performed at the Abbey Theatre on 13 January 1910. Molly directed the production and played Deirdre. It was published by the Cuala Press and included in the four-volume edition of *The Works of John M. Synge* published by Maunsel the same year. Despite this, and despite Yeats' continual praise and support, Synge's popularity remained an English and European phenomenon for some years, and not until long after Ireland had gained its independence were good words to be commonly said about *The Shadow of the Glen*, *The Playboy of the Western World* and *The Tinker's Wedding*. As Yeats remarked in his Preface to the last book Synge saw through the press, 'He was but the more hated because he gave his country what it needed.'

Molly Allgood as Deirdre, whose lament over Naisi in *Deirdre of the Sorrows* is Synge's lament for his own death

1871   16 April John Millington Synge born at Rathfarnham, near Dublin.

1872   Synge's father dies. Mrs Synge and her children move to Rathgar.

1885   Reads Darwin and suffers a crisis of faith.

1887   Begins studying the violin.

1888   Enters Trinity College, Dublin.

1890   Synge family move to Kingstown (now Dun Laoghaire).

1891   Awarded scholarship in counterpoint by the Royal Academy of Music, Dublin. Gains pass degree from Trinity College. Falls in love with Cherry Matheson.

1893   Studies music at Oberwerth, near Coblenz.

1894   Studies music at Würzburg. Summer in Ireland. Gives up music, and goes to Paris to teach English, study at the Sorbonne.

1895   Proposes to Cherry Matheson and is rejected. Begins *Vita Vecchia*. In Paris studies socialism and Irish antiquities and language.

1896   Meets W.B. Yeats in Paris. Visits Italy and meets Marie Zdanowska and Hope Rea. Proposes formally to Cherry Matheson and is rejected.

1897   Joins the Irish League in January but resigns in April. Studies mysticism and theosophy. Undergoes operation for growth in his neck. Begins *Etude Morbide*.

1898   19 January To Paris, wearing black wig. Attends lectures on Celtic civilization. Meets Margaret Hardon. 10 May–25 June, Synge's first visit to the Aran Islands. Visits Lady Gregory at Coole Park and meets Edward Martyn. Proposes to Margaret Hardon and is rejected.

1899   Visits Brittany and Aran Islands. Completes *Etude Morbide*.

1900   Third Aran visit. Begins *When the Moon Has Set*.

1901   Fourth Aran visit. Completes *The Aran Islands*, which is rejected by Grant Richards. Completes the two-act version of *When the Moon Has Set*, which is rejected by Lady Gregory for the Irish Literary Theatre.

1902   Writes *A Vernal Play, Luasnad, Capa and Laine, Riders to the Sea*, and *In the Shadow of the Glen*. Begins *The Tinker's Wedding*. Fisher Unwin rejects *The Aran Islands*.

1903   Visits West Kerry. *Riders to the Sea* rejected by *The Fortnightly* but published in *Samhain*. 8 October, first performance of *In The Shadow of the Glen*. Begins *The Well of the Saints*.

1904 Visits Mayo and revisits West Kerry. 25 February, first performance of *Riders to the Sea*. London performance of *Riders to the Sea* and *In the Shadow of the Glen*. Completes two-act version of *The Tinker's Wedding* and *The Well of the Saints*. *In The Shadow of the Glen* published by John Quinn in an edition of fifty copies in New York. Abbey Theatre born.

1905 4 February First performance of *The Well of the Saints*. Becomes a Director of the Irish National Theatre Society. *The Well of the Saints* translated into German, *In the Shadow of the Glen* into Czech. Visits 'Congested Districts' with Jack Yeats. Molly Allgood joins Abbey Theatre company. Third visit to West Kerry. *The Shadow of the Glen and Riders to the Sea* published in London by Elkin Mathews, *The Well of the Saints* by A.H. Bullen in London, and also by John Quinn in an edition of fifty copies in New York.

1906 Falls in love with Molly Allgood and they become secretly engaged. First draft of *The Playboy of the Western World*.

Abbey Theatre tours to England, Ireland and Scotland. Mrs Synge moves to Glendalough House, Glenageary, and Synge gives up his recently acquired flat in Rathgar to join her there.

1907 26 January First performance of *The Playboy of the Western World* causes riots in Dublin. Performed with great success in Oxford and London. Second operation for growth in neck. Begins *Deirdre of the Sorrows*. Synge suffers first indications of tumour in his side. *The Playboy of the Western World* published by Maunsel & Co., Dublin, *The Aran Islands* by Maunsel, and by Elkin Mathews, London.

1908 Exploratory surgery. Postpones marriage and continues working on *Deirdre of the Sorrows*. Synge's mother dies. His poems accepted for publication. *The Tinker's Wedding* published by Maunsel & Co., Dublin.

1909 24 March. Synge dies of Hodgkin's disease in the Elpis Nursing Home, Dublin.

ACKNOWLEDGMENTS

The present bibliographical portrait is largely based on material published in the biography *J.M. Synge 1871–1909* by David H. Greene and Edward M. Stephens (1959, Collier-Macmillan, New York) and in the four-volume *Collected Works of J.M. Synge* (1962-8, Oxford University Press, London) of which I was the General Editor.

I am indebted to Mrs Lily M. Stephens for enabling me to use family photographs; to Mr Liam Miller for much valuable advice and information and for the use of photographic material; to the National Library of Ireland for photographs from the Lansdowne Collection; and to other individuals and institutions acknowledged separately in the Notes on the Pictures.

Frontispiece: J.M. SYNGE in July 1906. A photograph taken in Edinburgh during the Abbey Theatre Company visit. *The Green Studio, Dublin.*

6 MAP OF IRELAND, showing the places associated with Synge's life and writings.

7 SYNGE'S BIRTHPLACE, 2 Newtown Villas, Rathfarnham, near Dublin. *Photo courtesy Liam Miller Esq.*

8 THE REV. ROBERT TRAILL, DD, MRIA, Rector of Schull, Co. Cork, Synge's maternal grandfather.

MRS ROBERT TRAILL, Synge's maternal grandmother.

JOHN HATCH SYNGE, Synge's father. *Courtesy Mrs Lily M. Stephens.*

9 J.M. SYNGE aged one year.

10 LEESON STREET, DUBLIN. Synge studied at No. 4 at Mr Herrick's Classical and English School. *Photo Irish Tourist Board.*

11 THE SYNGE FAMILY in 1885. *Courtesy Mrs Lily M. Stephens.*

12 'BOYCOTTING' A TRADESMAN, Co. Mayo. Cartoon from *The Illustrated London News* of December 1880. In 1880 Captain Boycott, an Irish landlord, was punished for his misdeeds by being totally ostracized by the community. No tradesman would serve him and no person speak with him. The incident gave rise to the verb, to boycott, and boycotting was frequently resorted to during the Irish Land War of the late nineteenth century and even later. *Photo Mansell Collection.*

13 CHARLES STEWART PARNELL in 1880. Parnell (1846–91) became interested in Irish politics in 1874 when he joined Isaac Butt's Home Rule Association and began to fight for the restoration of an Irish parliament. He was elected MP for County Meath in 1875 and from that time was a passionate fighter for social justice in Ireland, and for home rule. He fell from power in 1890 and died a year later having been regarded for over a decade as Ireland's 'Chief'. His downfall, caused partly by his being involved in an action for divorce, and thus losing the support of many of his followers and of the Church, was the cause of much bitter anticlericalism in Ireland. *Photo Mansell Collection.*

THE TRIPLE ALLIANCE. Cartoon from *The Weekly Freeman,* 1885–6. British Museum. *Photo Fleming.*

14, 15 EVICTION SCENES. The battering-ram was not only used to gain entrance to a cottage but also very frequently to aid in its complete destruction. *Photos National Library of Ireland.*

16 BAT, Plate 1 from Darwin's *The Zoology of the Voyage of H.M.S. Beagle under the*

Command of Captain Fitzroy. Part 1, *Fossil Mammalia, 1840.* British Museum. *Photo Fleming.*

17 THE DARGLE, Co. Wicklow. *Photo National Library of Ireland.*

18 DUBLIN NATURALISTS' FIELD CLUB, Announcement, 1886. *Courtesy Mrs Lily M. Stephens.*

DUBLIN NATURALISTS' FIELD CLUB, Membership list 1886. *Courtesy Mrs Lily M. Stephens.*

19 SYNGE'S VIOLIN AND BOW. *Photo Irish Tourist Board.*

BILL for violin lessons from Patrick Griffith, Synge's teacher, in 1888. *Courtesy Mrs Lily M. Stephens.*

20 TRINITY COLLEGE LIBRARY, Dublin. *Photo National Library of Ireland.*

21 TRINITY COLLEGE, Dublin. *Photo Mansell Collection.*

SYNGE'S LIBRARY CARD for Trinity College. *Courtesy Mrs Lily M. Stephens.*

ANTHONY TRAILL, MD, LLD, Synge's tutor and later, from 1904 to 1914, Provost of the College.

22 WEST DOOR of the Cathedral of Saints Peter and Paul, twelfth century, Glendalough, Co. Wicklow. *Photo Edwin Smith.*

23 THE CHURCHYARD, Glendalough, Co. Wicklow. *Photo Edwin Smith.*

24 CASTLE KEVIN, Co. Wicklow. *Courtesy Mrs Lily M. Stephens.*

25 CROSTHWAITE PARK, Kingstown (now Dun Laoghaire). *Photo National Library of Ireland.*

26 GLANMORE CASTLE, the Synge family seat in Co. Wicklow. *Courtesy Mrs Lily M. Stephens.*

THE COAT OF ARMS of the Synge family.

27 GLANMORE CASTLE, a distant view. *Courtesy Mrs Lily M. Stephens.*

28 A WICKLOW COTTAGE. 'At this season particularly when the first touch of autumn is felt in the evening air every cottage I pass by amongst the mountains, with an unyoked donkey cart lying [by] it and a hen going to roost on the three-legged pot beside the door, or perhaps a pool with rushes round it and a few children with the sadness of night coming upon them, makes me long that this twilight might be eternal and I pass these doors in endless pilgrimage.' *A Notebook of 1901. Courtesy Mrs Lily M. Stephens.*

31 FRÄULEIN VON EIKEN'S VISITING CARD. *Courtesy Mrs Lily M. Stephens.*

BILL from the von Eiken sisters. *Courtesy Mrs Lily M. Stephens.*

32 J.M. SYNGE. Photograph of 31 December 1895. *Courtesy Mrs Lily M. Stephens.*

33 PARIS, Avenue de L'Opéra. *Photo Roger-Viollet.*

34 PARIS, Bibliothèque Nationale. *Photo Mansell Collection.*

35 SÉBASTIEN FAURE (1858–1942), anarchist and author. Faure was the editor of the periodicals *l'Agitation* and *le Libertaire.* Among his most important works are *Authorité ou Liberté* (1891) and *Philosophie libertaire* (1895). *Photo Mansell Collection.*

SYNGE'S REGISTRATION CARD for the University of Paris. *Courtesy Mrs Lily M. Stephens.*

SYNGE'S READER'S CARD for the Bibliothèque Nationale from 11 January to 30 June 1900. *Courtesy Mrs Lily M. Stephens.*

36 ROME, Campo dei Fiori. *Photo Mansell/Anderson.*

37 FLORENCE. *Photo Mansell.*

HOPE REA'S VISITING CARD. *Courtesy Mrs Lily M. Stephens.*

38 DEMOCRATIC FEDERATION CARD designed by William Morris, whose works Synge studied in 1896 and whose socialist principles he found sympathetic. *Photo John Webb.*

39 W. B. YEATS (1865 to 1939), a photograph taken by T. W. Rolleston in his garden at Killarney. *Courtesy Lady Albery, daughter of T. W. Rolleston Esq.*

MAUD GONNE (1866–1953). Maud first met W. B. Yeats in 1889 and was associated with him in many of the activities of the Irish literary revival. She organized the Irish League in Paris and was for a time obliged to live in France rather than return to Ireland where she would have been arrested for her agitations on behalf of the oppressed peasantry. In 1903 she married Sean MacBride who had led the Irish Brigade in the Boer War. MacBride was courtmartialled and shot after the Easter Rising of 1916. Maud Gonne returned to Ireland after the war and was for a while imprisoned by the British. Her son, Sean, became the Minister for External Affairs in the Irish government of 1948. *Courtesy Mrs Lily M. Stephens.*

40 SYNGE in the grounds of Castle Kevin, 1897. *Courtesy Mrs Lily M. Stephens.*

41 SYNGE and 'Ben', 1897. *Courtesy Mrs Lily M. Stephens.*

42 GLENMALURE. *Photo Irish Tourist Board.*

43 GLEN MACNASS, Co. Wicklow. *Photo Irish Tourist Board.*

44 J. M. SYNGE. *Photo The Green Studio, Dublin.*

45 W. B. YEATS. Caricature by William Horton, 1898. *Photo Mansell Collection.*

GEORGE W. RUSSELL, called AE (1867–1935). A portrait by John Butler Yeats, 1903. AE was a poet, painter, journalist and social thinker who played a considerable part in the Irish renaissance. He made *The Irish Homestead,* of which he was editor from 1906 to 1923, an important intellectual and literary journal. Although a passionate nationalist, he believed England and Ireland to be economically interdependent and therefore did not join in the rising of Easter 1916. The most practical of economists and the most mystical of poets, he was the author of many volumes of essays and poetry. From 1923 to 1930 he was the editor of *The Irish Statesman. Photo the National Gallery of Ireland.*

47 ARAN ISLANDS, Kilronan Pier. *Photo the National Library of Ireland.*

48 THE PIER. A drawing by Jack B. Yeats for *The Aran Islands,* 1907 edition. *Courtesy Miss Anne Yeats.*

49 DUN CONOR, Inishmaan. *Photo Irish Tourist Board.*

50 COTTAGES ON INISHMAAN. *Photo Irish Tourist Board.*

51 THE CHURCH OF THE FOUR BEAUTIFUL PERSONS (Ceathair Aluinn). It was a story about the holy well, 'famous for cures of blindness and epilepsy', that provided a basic ingredient for *The Well of the Saints. Photo Irish Tourist Board.*

52 BRINGING IN THE SEAWEED FOR KELP, Inisheer. *Photo Irish Tourist Board.*

KELP-MAKING. A drawing by Jack B. Yeats for *The Aran Islands,* 1907 edition. *Courtesy Miss Anne Yeats.*

53 MAKING PAMPOOTIES. *Photo Radio Times Hulton Picture Library.*

54 ARAN ISLANDERS IN A CURAGH. *Photo Irish Tourist Board.*

55 CARRYING A CURAGH on Inisheer. *Photo Irish Tourist Board.*

56 AN OLD GALWAY WOMAN by her hearth. *Photo Mansell.*

58 LADY AUGUSTA GREGORY (1852–1923). Synge said of her *Cuchulain of Muir-themne*: 'This version of the epic tales relating to Cuchulain, the Irish mythical hero, should go so far to make a new period in the intellectual life of Ireland.' *Photo Mansell.*

59 COOLE PARK. *Photo Irish Tourist Board.*

61 SYNGE'S INITIALS on a tree at Coole Park. Also on the trunk may be seen George Bernard Shaw's large G.B.S., lower left-hand side, enclosed in a triangle, is AE (George Russell), S.O.C. (Sean O'Casey), and the initials of Kathleen Mansfield, Augusta Gregory and W.B. Yeats. *Photo Irish Tourist Board.*

62 GEORGE MOORE (1852–1933). Portrait by John Butler Yeats, 1905. Moore was the author of many novels and other prose works. He recorded his own involvement in the Irish revival in the three volumes of *Hail and Farewell: Ave, Salve and Vale* which were published in the years 1911 to 1914. *Photo National Gallery of Ireland, Dublin.*

EDWARD MARTYN (1859–1923). Cartoon from G. Plunkett's *To hold as 'twere*, Dundalgan Press, 1920. Martyn was a wealthy Catholic landlord devoted to the revival of Irish literature. He founded the annual Feis Ceoil (music festival), established the Palestrina Choir in Dublin and is credited with discovering the talent of John McCormack. He was one of the founders in 1898 of the Irish Literary Theatre, and his own plays include *The Heather Field, Maeve* and *The Dream Physician.*

63 TULLIRA CASTLE, home of Edward Martyn. *Photo Irish Tourist Board.*

64 FISHING BOATS, from Robert Flaherty's film 'Man of Aran'. *Courtesy Rank Organization.*

65 COTTAGE ON ARAN, from Robert Flaherty's film 'Man of Aran'. *Courtesy Rank Organization.*

67 SYNGE'S BLICKENSDORFER PORTABLE TYPEWRITER and its travelling case. Marked 'Made in the USA' though also marked 'Newcastle-on-Tyne', and of very simple construction. *Photo The Green Studio, Dublin.*

69 EARLY DRAFT of *When the Moon Has Set,* from Notebook 30. *Photo The Green Studio. Courtesy Mrs Lily M. Stephens.*

70 W.G. FAY (1872–1947). Producer and Stage Director of the Abbey Theatre. *Raymond Mander and Joe Mitchenson Theatre Collection.*

73 CABIN IN COUNTY WICKLOW. *Photo Radio Times Hulton Picture Library.*

75 DRAFT of *In the Shadow of the Glen,* from Box File E. *Photo The Green Studio. Courtesy Mrs Lily M. Stephens.*

76 STEPHEN MACKENNA (1888–1956), with William Gibson, President of the Gaelic League and (perhaps) Dominic Spring-Rice. Portrait by Clare Marsh. *Photo National Gallery of Ireland, Dublin.*

77 JOHN MASEFIELD (1878–1967), portrait by Jack B. Yeats, 1905. It was Masefield who caused the *Manchester Guardian* to commission a number of articles from Synge, the first published early in 1905. *Collection Mr and Mrs Burke Wilkinson, USA. Photo courtesy Victor Waddington.*

ARTHUR WILLIAM SYMONS (1865–1945), from the *Savoy*, No. 7, 1896. Symons was one of the most influential men of letters in the last years of the nineteenth century. He was an expert on contemporary French literature, a member of the Rhymers' Club and a regular contributor to the leading periodicals of the time. He collaborated with Aubrey Beardsley in producing the *Savoy* in 1896. His most important work is perhaps *The Symbolist Movement in Literature* (1899). He wrote many plays and books of poetry and published translations from six languages. He was a close friend of W.B. Yeats and was a supporter in the fight for the recognition of contemporary Irish writing.

78 JAMES JOYCE, 1895. *Croessman Collection, University of Southern Illinois Library.*

79 IRISH NATIONAL THEATRE SOCIETY PROGRAMME, October 1903. *Courtesy Mrs Lily M. Stephens.*

DOUGLAS HYDE (1860–1949), with A.P. Graves, 1894. Hyde was one of the leaders of the Irish literary revival. He published collections of folk-tales and folk-poetry, the most famous being the *Love Songs of Connacht*, with verse translations from the Irish by himself. He was the first President of the Gaelic League and in 1937 he became the first President of Eire. He was the author of a number of books in both Irish and English including *Beside the Fire* (1890), *The Story of Early Gaelic Literature* (1895) and *Literary History of Ireland* (1899). Synge greatly admired the language of his translations of *The Love Songs of Connacht,* and said of Hyde's Gaelic play, *The Twisting of the Rope* in 1901 that it 'gave a new direction and impulse to Irish drama, a direction towards which, it should be added, the thoughts of Mr W.B. Yeats, Lady Gregory and others were already tending.' *Photo T.W. Rolleston, Esq. Courtesy Lady Albery.*

80 FRANK FAY (1870–1903). Portrait by John Butler Yeats. The Abbey Theatre, Dublin. *Photo Dermot Barry.*

W.G. FAY (1872–1947). Portrait by John Butler Yeats. The Abbey Theatre, Dublin. *Photo Dermot Barry.*

81 MAIRE NI SHIUBLAIGH (Maire Walker). Portrait by John Butler Yeats. The Abbey Theatre, Dublin. *Photo Dermot Barry.*

82 PROGRAMME for the first production of two plays by W.B. Yeats and *In the Shadow of The Glen* by J.M. Synge. *Courtesy Mrs Lily M. Stephens.*

83 IN THE SHADOW OF THE GLEN: Maire ni Shiublaigh as Nora Burke in the first production.

IN THE SHADOW OF THE GLEN: W.G. Fay as the Tramp.

84 J.M. SYNGE. Drawing by John Butler Yeats, April 1905. *Courtesy Mrs Lily M. Stephens.*

85 ARTHUR GRIFFITH (1872–1922). Griffith, the Irish journalist and politician, became

137

deeply involved in the fight for Irish freedom shortly after the fall of Parnell. He was associated with the Gaelic League, the Young Ireland Society, Cumann na Gaedheal, and the Irish Republican Brotherhood. He founded the weekly paper, the *United Irishman* in 1899 and remained editor of it until 1906. In 1905 he founded the Sinn Fein party and in 1906 he resigned from the Irish Republican Brotherhood. When Dail Eireann was created as an independent parliament for Ireland in 1918, he became de Valera's Minister for Home Affairs. He was one of the signatories of the Irish Treaty of 1921, and in 1922 became the first President of the now legal Dail Eireann, but died before that first parliament of the new Irish Free State could gather together. *Photo Radio Times Hulton Picture Library.*

86 PROGRAMME for the first production of *Riders to the Sea*, given by the Irish National Theatre Society with *Deirdre* by AE.

87 RIDERS TO THE SEA. Scene from the 1906 production.

88 ABBEY THEATRE Announcement, 1904.

89 ABBEY THEATRE, Dublin. *Photo Mansell Collection.*

90 SYNGE'S FIRST BOOK: *In the Shadow of the Glen and Riders to the Sea*. Vigo Cabinet series, 1905. *Photo courtesy Liam Miller, Esq.*

91 MOLLY ALLGOOD. British Museum. *Photo Fleming.*

92 IN THE SHADOW OF THE GLEN in Czech. 1906 programme. *Courtesy Mrs Lily M. Stephens.*

93 C.P. SCOTT (1843–1932). Scott became editor of the *Manchester Guardian* in 1872.

He supported Gladstone's views on home rule for Ireland, and interested himself especially in the problems of the working class. He was a MP from 1895 to 1905, and played some part in the production of the Irish 'treaty' of 1921. He was throughout his life an avid supporter of all liberal causes and of Irish aspirations to independence. *Photo courtesy 'The Guardian'.*

JACK B. YEATS (1871–1957). Portrait by his father John Butler Yeats, *c*. 1895. Jack Yeats was the younger brother of W.B. Yeats and Ireland's greatest painter. He was also a playwright of originality and importance. His plays include *Apparitions* (1933) and *La La Noo* (1943). He is also the author of a number of idiosyncratic prose works including *Sligo* (1930), *The Amaranthers* (1936), and *The Careless Flower* (1947). A biography of him by Hilary Pyle was published in 1970 and his collected plays and prose are currently being edited by Robin Skelton. *Courtesy Victor Waddington Esq.*

94 J.M. SYNGE IN CONNEMARA. From a water-colour by Jack B. Yeats.

95 TWO CONNEMARA GIRLS. *Radio Times Hulton Picture Library.*

96 THE BLASKET ISLANDS, seen from Dun-quin. Synge visited the Blaskets in 1915, and his poem 'Beg-Inish' refers to the island of that name which is one of the group. *Photo Irish Tourist Board.*

97 CORRECTED PROOF of Synge's essay 'In West Kerry–Puck Fair' published in 1907 in *The Shanachie*. Trinity College, Dublin. *Photo The Green Studio.*

98 SARA ALLGOOD. Portrait by Sarah Purser. The Abbey Theatre, Dublin. *Photo Dermot Barry.*

99 MOLLY ALLGOOD (Maire O'Neill). Portrait by John Butler Yeats. Abbey Theatre, Dublin. *Photo Dermot Barry.*

100 RATHGAR ROAD, Dublin. *Photo Irish Tourist Board.*

101 J.M. SYNGE in July 1906. Photograph taken at Edinburgh during the Abbey Theatre Company's visit. *Photo The Green Studio. Courtesy Mrs Lily M. Stephens.*

102 WATERFORD, Co. Wicklow, Reginald's Tower. *Photo Radio Times Hulton Picture Library.*

103 BRAY, Co. Wicklow, The Promenade. *Photo Radio Times Hulton Picture Library.*

104 CHESTNUT TREES, Vence, etching by Edward Millington Synge (1860–1913). British Museum. *Photo Fleming.*

105 LADY GREGORY'S *Hyacinth Halvey,* production by the Abbey Theatre Company in 1906.

107 DRAFT of *The Playboy of the Western World. Photo The Green Studio. Courtesy Mrs Lily M. Stephens.*

108 LETTER from Jack B. Yeats to J. M. Synge, 1907, with a costume for *The Playboy of the Western World. Photo courtesy Liam Miller Esq.*

109 J.M. SYNGE at a rehearsal of *The Playboy of the Western World,* 24 January 1907. Drawing by John Butler Yeats.

110 THE END OF THE RACE, by Jack B. Yeats. *Courtesy Liam Miller Esq.*

112 NEWSPAPER REPORT of the opening of *The Playboy of the Western World, The Evening Herald,* 31 January 1907. *Courtesy Liam Miller Esq.*

114 W.B. YEATS: 'The Poet addressed the Audience'. Caricature by W. Orpen for *The Abbey Row.*

J.M. SYNGE: 'I don't care a rap!' Caricature by W. Orpen for *The Abbey Row. Courtesy Mrs Lily M. Stephens.*

115 ABBEY THEATRE PROGRAMME/'THE ABBEY ROW' COVERS. *Courtesy Mrs Lily M. Stephens.*

116 HEADLINES from the Dublin *Evening Telegraph* and *Evening Herald,* 29 November 1911. National Library of Ireland.

119 DRAFT OF 'ON A BIRTH-DAY', 1908. *Photo Green Studio, Dublin.*

121 CHARLES RICKETTS' COSTUME DESIGNS for the 1908 production of *The Well of the Saints. Photos courtesy Liam Miller Esq.*

123 POEMS AND TRANSLATIONS: Title-page, 1909. *Photo courtesy Liam Miller Esq.*

125 J.M. SYNGE in Coblenz, 1908. *Courtesy Mrs Lily M. Stephens.*

127 ST PATRICK'S CATHEDRAL, Dublin. *Photo Mansell Collection.*

128 EDWARD M. STEPHENS, Synge's nephew. *Courtesy Mrs Lily M. Stephens.*

129 MAUNSEL & COMPANY'S ANNOUNCEMENT of the publication of Synge's works in four volumes. James Joyce's *Dubliners* is announced on the same leaflet: *Dubliners,* however, was suppressed before publication. *Courtesy Mrs Lily M. Stephens.*

THE SYNGE FAMILY TOMB, Mount Jerome Cemetery, Dublin. *Photo Irish Tourist Board.*

130 MOLLY ALLGOOD in *Deirdre of the Sorrows. Photo Chancellor.*

SELECT BIBLIOGRAPHY

TEXTS
Robin Skelton (General Editor): *J. M. Synge: Collected Works*, Oxford University Press, 1961–8. The definitive edition of Synge's works in four volumes: Volume I, *Poems* (ed. Robin Skelton); Volume II, *Prose* (ed. Allan Price); Volumes III and IV, *Plays* (ed. Ann Saddlemyer).

BIOGRAPHIES
David H. Greene and Edward M. Stephens: *J. M. Synge 1871–1909*, Collier-Macmillan, New York 1959. The authorized biography by David H. Greene, making use of the long typescript biography by Edward M. Stephens as well as of Synge's notebooks and papers. It is the only full biography of Synge.

Maurice Bourgeois: *John Millington Synge and the Irish Theatre*, Constable, London 1913. A critical biography which, though frequently inaccurate, contains much perceptive criticism.

John Masefield: *John M. Synge: A Few Personal Recollections with Biographical Notes*, Cuala Press, Dublin 1915. A short but percipient memoir.

W. B. Yeats: *Synge and the Ireland of his Time*, Cuala Press, Dublin 1911. Contains Jack B. Yeats: 'With Synge in Connemara'.

Robin Skelton and David R. Clark (eds.): *Irish Renaissance*, Dolmen Press, Dublin 1965. Contains a collection of Synge's letters to Stephen MacKenna edited by Ann Saddlemyer.

Rev. Samuel Synge: *Letter to My Daughter: Memories of John Millington Synge*, Talbot Press, Dublin 1931. Impercipient, but not uninteresting.

CRITICAL WORKS
PARTICULAR
Francis J. Bickley: *J. M. Synge and the Irish Dramatic Movement*, Constable, London 1912.

P. P. Howe: *J. M. Synge: A Critical Study*, Secker, London 1912.

Daniel Corkery: *Synge and Anglo-Irish Literature*, Cork University Press 1931.

L. A. G. Strong: *John Millington Synge*, Allen and Unwin, London 1941.

Alan Price: *Synge and Anglo-Irish Drama*, Methuen, London 1961.

Ann Saddlemyer: *J. M. Synge and Modern Comedy*, Dolmen Press, Dublin 1967.

Robin Skelton: *The Writings of J. M. Synge*, Thames and Hudson, London; Bobbs Merrill, New York 1971.

GENERAL
Ernest A. Boyd: *The Contemporary Drama of Ireland*, Talbot Press, Dublin 1918.

Una M. Ellis-Fermor: *The Irish Dramatic Movement*, Methuen, London 1939.

W. G. Fay and Catherine Carswell: *The Fays of the Abbey Theatre*, Rich and Cowan, London 1935.

Lady Augusta Gregory: *Our Irish Theatre*, Putnam, New York 1913.

Peter Kavanagh: *The Story of the Abbey Theatre*, Devin-Adair, New York 1950.

Lennox Robinson: *Ireland's Abbey Theatre*, Sidgwick and Jackson, London 1951.

Page numbers in italics refer to the illustrations